LIFE ISSUES

GANGS

Ben Sonder

BENCHMARK BOOKS

MARSHALL CAVENDISH

NEW YORK

Published by Marshall Cavendish Corporation
99 White Plains Road
Tarrytown, NY 10591
USA

Library of Congress Cataloging-in-Publication Data

Sonder, Ben.
    Gangs / by Ben Sonder.
        p.   cm. — (Life issues)
    Includes bibliographical references and index.
    Summary: Discusses youth gangs, including information about
their appeal to young people, the problems of gang-related violence
and drugs, and how to get out and stay out of gangs.
    ISBN 0-7614-0021-4 (lib. bdg.)
    1. Gangs—United States—Juvenile literature. 2. Juvenile delinquency—
United States—Juvenile literature.   [1. Gangs.]
    I. Title. II. Series.
    HV6439.U5S62 1996
    364.3'6'—dc20

                                            95-11178
                                              CIP
                                              AC

Printed and bound in the United States of America

Produced by Jacquerie Productions

Photographic Note
Several persons depicted in this book are photographic models; their appearance in these photographs is solely to
dramatize some of the situations and choices facing readers of the Life Issues series.

Photo Credits
Hazel Hankin: p. 18
Impact Visuals: p. 4, 35, 48, 84 (Andrew Lichtenstein); 6 (Catherine Smith); 8, 25, 72, 79 (Jim Tynan);
        10, 15, 21, 40, 42, 53, 54, 67, 87 (Donna DeCesare); 12, 51 (Chris Takagi); 22 (Jack Kurtz); 28 (Lonny Shavelson);
        30 (Ted Soqul); 32 (Donna Binder); 38 (Lisa Terry); 62 (Hazel Hankin); 70 (E. Charrington); 80 (Jeff Scott);
        82 (Tom McKitterick)
The Picture Cube: p. 60 (C. Blankenhorn); 65 (Jeffrey Dunn)
Frances M. Roberts: p. 44
Swanstock: p. 46 (Paul D'Amato)
Sygma: p. 57 (D. Kuroda)

Cover photo: Impact Visuals (Jeff Scott)

The producer would like to thank Capt. Frank Messar for reviewing this manuscript.

CONTENTS

PROLOGUE

This book is about gangs—their strengths, their weaknesses, their appeal, and their dangers. If you don't know anything about gangs, it will explain to you why gangs are formed and how they function. It will also offer you some sound advice for dealing with them if that occasion occurs.

If you already know about gangs and think they are "cool," this book will challenge your assumptions. Using numerous stories from real life, it will take you inside the world of gangs and show you how they have affected gang members, their friends, their enemies, and their families. If you've had a taste of gang life and now want out, this book could possibly help you. At the very least, it should help you clarify your feelings about the gang experience.

More and more, gangs are becoming a part of growing up in America. This used to be the case mostly in urban areas of the country. But lately, gang life has reached small towns as well. The reasons for this are many. Until they are fully understood, the popularity of gangs and the dangerous consequences of gang life are likely to increase.

Gangs come in all shapes, sizes, styles, and colors. Some are based on ethnic background and some are ethnically mixed. Some are all-boy gangs or all-girl gangs. Some admit people of both sexes. Some stress violence while others try to avoid violence and focus on support. Some encourage sharing and equality, whereas others are ruthless dictatorships that treat their members cruelly. This book has tried to discuss as many different types of youth gangs as possible. All of the personal stories are true, although in most cases names have been changed to protect the privacy of individuals. In some cases, the names of the gangs and the identifying clothing they wear have been changed as well.

The world of youth gangs is often one of extreme decisions, heart-breaking loss, and dramatic violence. Some of the accounts of gang life in this book may be hard for you to take. They are here not to shock, but to provide a balanced picture of the youth gang experience. Youth gangs are a reality that must be clearly faced.

1

FROM GROUP TO GANG

My G's are my family.
—Marla, age 15

Welcome to Little Rock, Arkansas, in the center of America's heartland. Population: 177,000. Meet Little Rock's youth gangs. Total number: 100, including the Crips and Bloods from L.A. and the Folk from Chicago. Turn on the Little Rock news: There's a good chance you'll see the aftermath of a drive-by shooting, or hear about the latest arrest of a teen gang member. Talk to Little Rock residents: You'll hear the fear, the worry, and the disbelief in their voices.

In the past few years, Little Rock stopped being a small, sleepy city and inherited all the problems of America's big inner cities. The moment that the Crips and the Bloods from L.A. and the Folk from Chicago came South and started branches of their "nations," gangs became a reality in Little Rock. Many of Little Rock's gangs are "equal opportunity employers." They are multiracial, their members range in age from 11 to 39, and some of them accept both boys and girls.

Meet Marla. She's 15, white, a native of Little Rock. She just got "beat in" to a Little Rock branch of the Folk Nation known as the Hoovers. The Hoovers accept all races and both males and females. Getting "beat in" is an initiation into the gang that consists of savage blows from fellow gang members, followed by hugs. The Hoovers use the sign of the pitchfork as

When does hanging out with a group of friends turn into being part of a gang? The turning point often comes when the group consciously begins to exclude some people.

their logo. So Marla will be getting her pitchfork tattoo soon. The tattoo is made by heating a fork on a stove until it gets red-hot and then searing the flesh with the prongs to make a pitchfork shape. Once you are in the gang, there is supposed to be no way to get out—except by dying.

According to Marla, this process of becoming a "G," or gang member, is "not just about getting your ass kicked. It's all about love." Love is something Marla probably needs a lot of. When she talks about her childhood, she doesn't mince words. She was physically and sexually abused by her family, taken away from them for a while. Now she rarely thinks of them, except with contempt and with a wild feeling of pleasure at not needing them at all.

"My G's help me out," she says. "My G's are the only ones who taught me to love. The Folk is our unity, the Hoovers are our family." Marla says she'd be willing to die for the Hoovers if it came down to it. She feels loved and fearless, free and superior.

Like most gangs, Marla's gang has enemies. One of the main enemies of the Little Rock Hoovers is the Bloods. The Bloods are a Little Rock branch of the enormous network of gangs called Bloods that flourishes in Los Angeles. They are mostly black. The Hoovers call the Bloods "the Slobs" and spend a lot of time talking about "blowing them away." They talk about it righteously, as if the

This young woman is part of a Hispanic gang in Los Angeles. She forms a gang hand sign with her right hand.

Bloods have started all the trouble in Little Rock and the Hoovers are just trying to defend their turf. But other inhabitants of Little Rock feel differently. They're tired of the question of "who started it first." They just want the violence to stop. Gang violence isn't just killing gang members. Drive-by shootings have killed children and infants sitting in their living rooms. Shoppers have been held up at cash machines by G's from most of the hundred gangs trying to get money to buy guns.

One person with a bird's-eye view of the gang problem in Little Rock is the city coroner, the man who puts a tag on the toe of every dead body the police bring in. For the last few years, he's been noticing that the bodies are getting younger and younger. The fact bothers him so much that he's made up some posters with pictures of the teenage corpses. He drives from neighborhood to neighborhood showing off the posters. When young kids pick out friends or relatives from the photos, he points out how senseless the loss of lives is becoming. He pleads with them to stop. But from the way he speaks, he seems to understand what the kids are getting out of membership in a gang. He knows they want a sense of belonging, family, love, and strength. They just don't know how to get it any other way.

WHAT IS A GANG?

gang \'gan\ *n* (1): a set of articles: OUTFIT (2): a group of persons having informal and usu. close social relations <have the *gang* over for a party> (3): a group of persons working to unlawful or antisocial ends [from *Webster's New Collegiate Dictionary*]

A gang is a group, just like a family, a football team, or even a nation. The word can be used to describe any group of mutually supportive people who work together for a common goal. If you and your close friends form a network that helps those of you who are down, if you often party together, if you're ready to stick together against enemies, then all of you already know a lot about the dynamics of a gang.

Gang. The word sends shivers of fear through those who live in places like Little Rock. If you are one of these people, you may already have lost a brother or sister to a drive-by shooting or heard streets echo with gunfire. In fact, at this very moment you yourself may be being harassed by a gang or under pressure to become a member. Some aspects of gang life may even seem appealing—the automatic group of friends, the protection from enemies, the partying.

Or, if you have already become a gang member, you may be experiencing some of the thrills you were promised. Wearing the colors and gear of the gang probably gives you a feeling of belonging and status. It may be easier to get dates and you may be getting invited to a lot of parties. If your gang is involved

Gang members spend a lot of time hanging out with each other in the neighborhood. These members of the Mara Salvatrucha or MS gang in Los Angeles show off their gang tattoos and hand signs.

in defending turf and is succeeding at it, it probably feels good to be able to make others do what you want them to do. Your membership in a gang may even be making you richer, although you probably wouldn't want anyone not involved to know much about the sources of that money.

There's a good chance that you like your gang better than your teachers or your family. Your gang leader may seem a lot more accepting and a lot less unfair than your own parents. Your gang "family" may seem warmer and more fun-loving than your own family of birth. Maybe you feel your homies (short for "homeboys," fellow gang members) are really "there for you." Membership in your gang may also be making you feel prouder about your ethnic background, when before it seemed as if the whole world was saying your people were second-rate.

But what if you've been in a gang for a long time? At this point, there's a fair chance that the support and the thrills are starting to be outweighed by the costs. Perhaps you've already served time in a youth detention facility or even

DEFINING GANGS

A gang differs from a group of friends or associates because its members' aims partly involve illegal or antisocial acts. Aside from this one common characteristic, gangs differ widely in their size, group goals, rules, and habits. We can, however, identify some common types of gangs:

The neighborhood gang, or "crew." Usually a small group of young people from the same neighborhood, crews loosely band together for having fun, offering each other support, or acting as a group to solve common problems. Crews usually start informally. The same group of friends who spend a lot of time together begin to develop certain habits of interaction. When a crew starts seeing itself as opposed to other groups in the neighborhood and takes hostile action, or when it becomes involved in illegal activities, it can be considered a gang.

The street gang. This type of gang is usually larger and more highly organized. It may involve a whole neighborhood or a larger part of the community. Authority is usually in the hands of a few powerful individuals at the top. Conflicts with other large gangs are common. So are illegal businesses. These youth gangs sometimes develop relationships to adult criminal operations. They may carry on recruiting activities as well.

The prison gang. Several religious and fraternal organizations were originally started in prison. Some of these, though not all, have taken on the characteristics of gangs. Gangs in prison provide protection, distribute drugs or illegal goods, and provide peer counseling and recruitment for activities in the outside world. Sometimes these gangs are branches of gangs that already exist on the streets. In other cases, they began in prison, then continued their activities in the outside world once members are released. In still other cases, they function only in prison.

an adult prison because you got arrested. Or you may have been beaten up, stabbed, or shot by members of a rival gang. In fact, the violence against you could have come from within your gang, because you were accused of betraying an oath or because you were caught in the midst of a struggle for power. You may have become addicted to drugs, although you originally only started to handle them for sale to others. Or you may suddenly be coming to the realization that those street-fighting skills you are so proud of were sharpened at the expense of people who weren't even enemies.

Deaths from gang violence have risen sharply in recent years. The victims are usually young people. Here the grandmother of a 16-year-old murder victim participates in an anti-gang vigil.

Whatever is happening to you, similar things are happening to many others. In news articles, TV programs, and books, the stories of gangs are being told. What is especially shocking is that these stories are remarkably the same. High school students who belong to gangs tell it again and again: how they first got pressured or lured into a gang; or how what started as a bunch of good friends suddenly grew out of control, got wilder; how the growth into a full-fledged gang eventually cost them the love of friends and family.

Sometimes, long-term, dyed-in-the-wool gang members talk boastfully to reporters about the ways they have changed. They explain why a large part of their wardrobe has become a uniform—designed to announce to everybody who they are and whose orders they follow. They explain how powerful they feel because they are always carrying a weapon. They explain why gang membership has become an entire way of life, why they constantly have to scan the school corridor or sports field for enemies. Or how the neighborhood is now a battlefield that needs twenty-four-hour defense.

And then sometimes their families are interviewed by reporters. Sobbing parents tell how they lost their 14-year-old to bullets during a gang-bang. Grandparents give testimony to their grandchildren's former good character before disbelieving judges. Girls talk about the ways they were mistreated by an all-male gang and then forced to keep quiet about it.

LOOKING AT TODAY'S YOUTH GANGS

If you are a long-term member of a gang, you may be wondering how all the exciting things about gangs that first attracted you gradually turned sour. How did the first definition of a gang—with all its positive qualities of supportiveness and togetherness—become the nightmare second definition? What defines today's youth gangs and what makes them so explosive? Many of them started as a small group of friends who came together for good reasons. Even when some of these groups became full-fledged violent gangs, they did not lose all of their positive qualities. Almost every characteristic that they share has a bad side and a good side. In fact, every gang—or for that matter, every group—you could think of seems to have had a beginning based on positive impulses, a golden period when members benefited, and a decline where things got out of hand. Gang members offer many explanations for why they joined their gang. The reasons may sound positive at first, but later they become excuses for destruction and bad faith.

Survival. It is no accident that gangs often form in the context of urban poverty. In violence-ridden neighborhoods with few services, a group often fares better than an individual. Members of gangs share food, clothing, and shelter. They are bound by honor to protect each other and their turf against enemies. Sometimes gang membership seems the best option for making a good living.

FEMALE GANGS

Female gang members have existed as long as gangs have. They are still a minority, but one that has been growing steadily. In New York City in 1980, 10 percent of gang members were female. No one knows the exact national percentage of females now but many experts suspect it to be well over 10 percent.

Some female gang members belong to all-female gangs that have their own codes of behavior, insignia, and special operations. Other girls are members of gangs that accept both females and males. Girls' involvements in gangs vary widely. In some, they must play the double role of gang-banger and traditional sex object, or girlfriend. In others, they share the same rights, responsibilities, and dangers as the boys. Many all-girl gangs arose as "protection posses," groups of girls who banded together in dangerous neighborhoods to avoid the threat of violence or rape. However, the current trend of some female gangs more and more resembles the model of male gang-banging, in which turf wars, violence for profit, and all-powerful leaders dominate the activities of the group.

Unfortunately, survival is today one of the most overused excuses of violent gang members. It's often used to describe risky activities that actually put an individual in great danger. What is considered survival in a gang has become strictly defined. Thus, getting help from teachers or social service agents may be considered "copping out." But robbing or drug dealing may be labeled as survival.

Self-esteem. People often join groups to boost their self-esteem. Urban ghetto life can be a constant source of disappointment and failure. Prejudice against minorities has left some American young people with resentments and inferiority complexes. Groups of similar people boost self-esteem. A gang is an automatic group of friends. Because gang membership is often based on race, class, and neighborhood, your fellow gang members are likely to have a lot in common. The problem is that most gangs have other things in common that lower self-esteem. Getting beaten, arrested, or spending time in detention can be a humiliating experience. Getting older but having no other skills than those for street survival can make you feel inadequate. What starts out as self-esteem often ends up as an even deeper sense of inferiority.

Family. A large proportion of youths in violent gangs today either come from broken homes or from homes where there is an atmosphere of disharmony and violence. Gangs are substitute families. They offer new members the promise of unconditional love or strict discipline, either of which they may not be getting from their parents. Gang leaders play the roles of fathers and mothers, and older gang members are supposed to offer counsel and support to newcomers. It's just too bad that gang members bring their problems of low self-esteem and dysfunctional families with them. Since gang leaders are often the product of abusive parents, they begin repeating that abusive behavior with their charges. Since people who join gangs often have low self-esteem, the bonding offered by gangs often degenerates into petty quarrels. Sometimes gangs splinter into smaller groups that fight each other. At other times they take out their rage and low self-esteem on other minorities, who become their victims.

Ethnic identity. The prevalence of gangs in the United States is proof of America's ongoing racism. There often is no other way for members of a minority to explore their native culture than to band together in a gang that tries to shut out and belittle the rest of mainstream America. When television, film, and other media promote only the values of one ruling culture, people of other cultures become alienated and retreat into their own private worlds. In some ways, gangs are no different than other youth organizations based on ethnicity. But what does make them different is that the ethnicity they are promoting has been severely rejected by other Americans. Thus, gang members are banding together not only in solidarity but in anger. Under such conditions, ethnic consciousness can become defensive and vengeful. It can lead to boasts of superiority and contempt for other ethnic groups.

Most gangs are exclusively male, although some gangs admit women as equal members. There are also some all-girl gangs, such as this one in East Los Angeles.

Power and entitlement. This factor is related to the survival factor. Even a person who is fed three meals a day and given shelter may feel like a loser. If symbols of status always seem out of reach, daydreams of "making it" may become a preoccupation. Gang members are often ambitious people who fantasize about high achievements. Gangs offer the possibility of quickly winning superficial symbols of status and power: expensive cars, flashy jewelry, "fly" clothes, and attractive lovers. The slow way of winning these prizes—years of education and striving for acceptance in the corporate world—may appear permanently out of reach.

Rites of passage. It's common for people to enter gangs during the adolescent years. This is because the dares and challenges of the gang lifestyle are a convenient way to prove your selfhood or maturity. Gang members learn to compete with each other and with other gangs for mastery. Many gangs have initiation ceremonies in which a new member has to beat up a rival, suffer a ritual knife cutting, or walk along the edge of a roof without falling. The experience of "winning" may be just what a growing person is looking for. In fact, competitive sports, dating rituals, and other challenging activities of young adulthood have always provided the rites of passage that an adolescent needs. But most gang-style rites of passage are of the high-risk sort. They may give a rush of pleasure to the participant who succeeds, but they can also kill or maim.

WHAT YOU SHOULD KNOW ABOUT GANGS

More than half of Americans between the ages of 10 and 17 say that fear of violence is their greatest worry.

• Fifty-six percent of the same age group worry about a member of their family becoming a victim of violent crime.

• One-third of the same age group said they know where to get a gun.

• Twenty-four percent said they had been threatened by someone holding a gun or knew someone who had.

• Approximately 100,000 guns and 600,000 knives are brought to U.S. schools every day.

• About 3 million thefts or destruction of property occur on school campuses each year.

Displacement of anger. This category covers a host of problems. Young people who join gangs may be secretly angry at themselves for living in poverty or not succeeding at school. They may resent the fact that members of the opposite sex don't seem to take any interest. Or they may have homosexual impulses that lead to feelings of shame or self-revulsion. Finally, they may harbor a secret resentment against a parent, grandparent, or sibling that would cause too much guilt to admit outright. Half-acknowledged feelings can find their expression in gang-banging. The aggressive thrill of fighting for turf, preying upon the helpless, or destroying property may express these secret resentments that a person may not even be aware of harboring. The only drawback is that such behavior never puts a person in touch with the problem that is causing the anger. The problem is never solved.

Lack of alternatives. Some people are in dangerous gangs simply because they got trapped in them. This happens as a result of many complicated factors. Initially, they may have been attracted to gang life because of the survival opportunities, chances for power and money, or sense of belonging it seemed to promise. Or they may have felt they had no choice. It was a question of joining the gang or becoming one of its victims. On the other hand, they may have had no intention of becoming part of a dangerous gang. A simple group of best friends may have grown into something out of their control. Feelings of loyalty to friends may be keeping them from dropping out. Threats of violence against their leaving the gang may be keeping them in as well.

In any of these reasons, we might be able to identify the subtle turning point at which a support group becomes a dangerous gang. Groups go bad at that point when the goals of the group endanger the safety and welfare of its individual members, even if the goals seemed positive in the beginning. But when this turning point occurs, few gang members are free enough or clear-thinking enough to do something about it. In fact, tyranny of the ever-more-powerful group over the individual is the major hallmark of every dangerous youth gang.

2

STORY OF A GANG

We just wanted to feel safe in our neighborhood.
—Felipe, age 15

New gangs often don't start with bad intentions. Many gangs started as a necessary support group of friends. The Diamond Heights Gang is a good example. It started innocently enough. A few friends decided they were sick of having to feel afraid in their own neighborhood.

At 15, Felipe Ulloa Velez, a Chicano living in San Francisco's Diamond Heights neighborhood, and his three best friends—Johnny Boy, Whisper, and Spits—all felt they had the same problem. The white guys in the neighborhood, whom Felipe and his friends called "the neighboring Nazis," were picking on them. They were attacking them with racial slurs and sometimes even with fists. As a solution, the four friends decided to form a formal support group, which would later become known as the Diamond Heights Gang. At first, their crew was small, just a few of their friends, but then suddenly it began to blossom. The four friends discovered that there were lots of other kids who felt the way they did. Felipe tells it like this:

> It was weird. As soon as we told a few people, it was like targeted advertising and caused people to flock to this store outlet where we were hanging. All of a sudden. Out of the woodwork. They all

Elaborate gang graffiti is an expression of pride in the group—and also indicates the boundaries of the gang's territory.

heard about four cats that were holding onto their 'hood. We held back several years about who we let in—we were very selective. But it grew and grew to be about sixty members. Finally it became a mixed group. It had lots of us Chicanos but we let in other people, too.

The effect of the Diamond Heights Chicano support group was just what Felipe and his friends had desired. The harassment from the white kids was stopped dead. But that wasn't all. Felipe's gang began to get a certain reputation. Eventually, even kids who had had no trouble in the neighborhood wanted to join.

Why did kids who had no problems want to join? If you think about it, you'll probably find the answer in your own mind and heart. The Diamond Heights Gang was about being proud. It made a bold statement: Diamond Heights belonged just as much (or even more) to the Chicanos and other non-whites as it did to the whites. This rally for pride appealed to a lot of the neighborhood homies. And though Felipe was only 14, he proved a terrific "big brother." Soon every boy wanted to be a member of this new street "family."

New member homies weren't the only people Felipe's gang began to attract. The Diamond Heights Gang also began to attract girls. "The girls from different schools came out to find out what we were about and they liked it," explains Felipe. "Their boyfriends didn't, but we just laughed at them."

It may have been precisely at this point that the Diamond Heights crew changed from a neighborhood support group into something more uncontrollable, something like a gang. Now it was becoming a group of people using the power of their numbers not just to protect themselves, but to get what they wanted. Unfortunately, increased membership, more status, and adoring females turned out to be harder to handle than the gang had bargained for.

It ended up that we had two, three, four, five people in each high school. It started causing animosity. Most of us weren't in school anymore, but a lot of us would go just to hang out and before you know it, there'd be twenty or thirty of us hanging out in the schoolyard. And we had the girls. So then everybody else started hating us. Nobody wanted to kick back with us. We couldn't go nowhere.

What happened to Felipe's gang is bound to happen to almost any growing power base. It's something to keep in mind if you are thinking about forming a support group. The principle works as follows: the more power a group has, the more enemies it generates. For a time, those enemies may be too powerless to endanger the group. But sooner or later the balance of power shifts. Felipe's group started making enemies as soon as it took pleasure in "stealing" girlfriends. New members were forming small power bases in high schools and neighborhoods that had never had any problems. Now that there were people who were throwing their weight around, they became something to oppose. Schools and neighborhoods that had been peaceful, weren't anymore.

According to Felipe, things could have been ironed out if something else hadn't happened. What happened was that kids who were much younger than the 14-, 15-, and 16-year-olds of the Diamond Heights Gang began looking up to them as heroes. "They'd look at us and we'd be all cholo'ed out [all dressed up in the colors and gear of the gang], with half a baseball bat in our pants," Felipe explains. "The little kids wanted to go, too."

Letting a younger crowd into the Diamond Heights Gang turned out to be a near-fatal mistake. Some of the 14-year-olds in the gang might not have had perfect judgment, but they had a basic street sense. A lot of the younger kids didn't. As leader of the Diamond Heights Gang, Felipe decided that these junior members needed to be organized into a subgroup, which came to be called the Lower Heights Crew. In doing this he hoped to satisfy the little kids' need for belonging and status without involving them too much in any of the older members' risky business. He wanted to give them the "image" without giving them too much responsibility.

For a while, this solution worked. The little kids strutted around the neighborhood imitating the clothes and gestures and walking style of the older guys. But then . . .

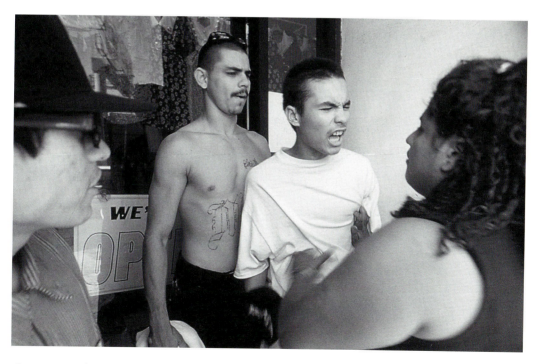

Once gangs become active in a neighborhood, the streets usually change for the worse. Confrontation and violence can take over.

Next thing you know, the little kids begin to get jumped. Then they start getting in every fight they can get their hands on. As soon as something's in the air and they hear the rumor, there they are on the bus and ready to go. Then one day it happens: one of our guys gets stabbed in the heart. Again, a little guy—a Lower Heights member. Stabbed at Silver and Mission. Midgets of another rival gang stabbed our friend in the heart. He ran home on adrenaline and collapsed in front of his house. But he lived. Medics came in five minutes and said it was a miracle he lived.

Young children naturally look up to older boys and want to imitate them. Some gangs admit kids as young as 10 as "junior" members.

What would you do if a group you had started for support eventually led to the near-death of one of your people—somebody who was still just a young child? Would you pack in the group and decide that the whole thing had been a mistake? Or would you try to correct the problem by seeking revenge? Felipe tried the second solution:

> You see, people started blaming me for starting the little-guys gang. So I went to see the kid and he tells me the name of the person with the knife. A couple days later—by a big coincidence—we're only two, three blocks along on the bus, and there's the dude did it walking with his girl. I go, "Lemme talk to him first." He was with his girl and one of the rules was not to do anything in front of girls. He didn't even notice that all of us were behind him. Younger kids made a big circle around him . . .

The next split second might have changed Felipe's life forever. Up until that moment, he had had every intention of finding a way to avenge the stabbing of his little homie. But, at that moment, something must have clicked. In his mind's eye he must have seen the future: an endless circle of killings for revenge and the endless paybacks. So Felipe cut his enemy a deal:

> I said, "I'll save your life and save us a lot of trouble. You do one thing for me. Tell me the truth what happened." The dude said he didn't mean to and started crying. Others were grabbing at him. But I held them off. "We're not gonna jump you, but you jump yourself out. If I hear you're hanging out with them, these guys will catch you." So he went and got himself jumped out. To tell you the truth, if the guy had not been with his old lady, he would have got massacred. I would have been an accessory to a murder. [To "jump yourself out" means to ask to be let out of gang membership. It often involves taking a beating from fellow gang members.]

A BRUSH WITH DEATH

Felipe's close brush with murder wasn't the only trouble he got into. For two years he and his homeboys had been picking on a shell-shocked Vietnam vet who lived near their junior high school. They would see him in the morning in his yard, half dressed but wearing combat boots, singing *The Star-Spangled Banner* to the flag he'd put up. They'd hurl insults and he'd shout back.

One day Felipe jumped over the fence and into the vet's yard out of curiosity. He wanted to peek into the man's house. He felt an arm pull him from behind. The next thing he knew, he was rolling on the ground in a bloody fight with the vet. Some of his crew, who were in the schoolyard, noticed what was going on and jumped over the fence, too. The vet was badly injured and Felipe was arrested. The entire incident was blamed on him, but Felipe refused to give the names of the friends who had helped him. So Felipe alone had to go into a juvenile detention facility for a few months. At the time, he was proud of this because, "It gained me a rep as not being a snitch."

Felipe didn't really leave the gang. Instead, the gang grew naturally into something more peaceful as the members became older. Felipe was one of the first to announce that he didn't want to be in situations where people could be hurt or killed anymore. By the time he reached 20, he was out for good. Now in his mid-twenties, he lives peacefully with a wife and two children and has a full-time job. Some of his old gang buddies have moved into well-paying jobs. One is the vice-president of a computer company and another is an auto transmission mechanic. The crowd still gets together, but mostly for peaceful pursuits, like collecting, rebuilding, and riding antique cars.

Felipe Velez may have got out of gang life , but gang life never got out of him. He still speaks with wistful excitement about "those days." However, because he's an intelligent person with a new style of life to protect, he indulges his old gang instincts by teaching young Chicanos and helping out some of the younger kids in his neighborhood.

WHAT WENT WRONG WITH THE DIAMOND HEIGHTS GANG?

Felipe's story has a happy ending, but lots of these stories haven't. He barely made it. If he hadn't decided to give the knife attacker a chance, where would he be now? If the Vietnam vet had died from the beating, what would have happened to Felipe?

You might not want to take such chances when it comes to living your life. You probably won't take them if you understand what you are doing and why you are doing it.

Let's take a close look at the Diamond Heights Gang and how it came to be. The gang started for survival. Felipe and his four friends were being unfairly oppressed by a few white neighbors who thought they owned the streets. A support group to defend against the oppressors might have been a good idea. But this group could have begun with rules that would have kept it from getting out of hand. In the first place, it could have limited its members to those few people who were being harassed by the white guys.

When a gang turns to weapons for a sense of power and protection, that gang has become corrupt and dangerous.

Felipe and his friends decided to handle their own self-defense needs because they wanted to be self-reliant. This was probably good for their sense of worth and their need to think of themselves as capable people. But occasionally a person needs help from somebody with more influence. Maybe there was a teacher, priest, cop, father, mother, or big brother who could have put a stop to the white kids' harassment. And then again, maybe there wasn't.

In many ways, the Diamond Heights Gang grew into a family. They shared common goals and common pleasures. The older, more experienced members were supposed to make the rules and offer the protection. Kids whose families were not functioning very well probably got a lot out of hanging with the Diamond Heights crew. The older gang members were probably really sincere in wanting to be good "big brothers." But the Diamond Heights Gang didn't have the discipline or the power to bring up a family on the street. Who does? The street is too unpredictable—much more so than the school or the home. No matter how much they wanted to protect their junior members, there was no way of keeping them out of trouble.

WHAT CAN HAPPEN

Because gang-related violence has skyrocketed, many U.S. judges have raised the penalties for gang-related crime committed by teenagers. Age matters less these days than the severity of the crime. Consider this example:

On February 17, 1995, in the Chicago area, a 16-year-old gang member was sentenced to forty years in prison for the shooting of a 20-year-old mother. The defendant, Javier Ureste, had fired six shots from a handgun at a group of gang members. The bullets missed, but one of them hit the 20-year-old woman in the heart. Ureste's attorney had asked for the minimum sentence of twenty years because of his client's youth. The maximum he could have gotten was sixty years. Upon hearing the sentence of forty years, Ureste burst into violent sobbing.

Of course, it's no surprise that the junior members *wanted* to get in trouble. All the senior members did was boast about how much power they had. Even their cholo look and their bat weapons were a way of bragging. Wanting to act grown up, the little kids imitated what they saw. And all they saw were cool clothes, weapons, and pride in fighting skills. It's true that a gang offers a lot of things found in the ideal family. But the skills it knows how to teach just don't go very far. The senior members of the Diamond Heights Gang just couldn't offer their little brothers much.

Even with all of these lacks, the Diamond Heights Gang might never have gotten into the trouble it did. Its biggest mistake was that it became corrupt. That moment in which it turned a defensive operation into an offensive one is the moment that the violent gang really is born. When the Diamond Heights Gang started using their new power to pull girls away from their boyfriends, they began using their clout in an unjust manner. And when they began using their power to ridicule a mentally ill veteran, they had sunk to the level of the white kids who had oppressed them in the first place. This was the moment when the Diamond Heights Group turned from a support group into a group of hypocritical outlaws.

The story of the Diamond Heights Gang is a lesson for anybody who finds himself in a similar situation. If you are getting harassed by other people in the neighborhood, get help. If help comes by forming a support group, make sure the rules of that group are hard and fast. If your group feels like a big family, honestly ask yourself what that family really has to offer. And if your group was formed to right a wrong, dump it the moment you see it is slipping into the errors it was designed to correct.

3

THE LURE OF THE RACE GANG

*They're just animals. We should send them
back where they came from.*
—Jimmy, age 17

Did you ever dream about re-making the world so that it would become a place filled with your beliefs, your people, and your lifestyle? Many gangs based on the idea of a shared race or ethnic background are about private worlds in which those identities rejected by mainstream America can reign. Some of these "realities" created by gang life are all-black or all-Latin. Others are fantasy-attempts to create an all-white world in which there are no blacks or Latins or Asians. However, all race gangs share one thing in common: the defensive idea that their culture is superior, special, and misunderstood.

June 13, 1992, was a big day for certain residents of Birmingham, Alabama. Three white-supremacist organizations united to march through downtown to show the world that "white skin rules." Most of the younger marchers had the close-cropped hair of skinheads; they belonged to the Confederate Hammer Skinheads of America, an all-white gang with branches throughout the country. The other two groups participating were formed of older people. They were the National Aryan Front and the Aryan White Knights, which are branches of the Ku Klux Klan. All three groups had come to Birmingham from surrounding states in an act of "solidarity."

Race plays a major role in gangs. The boys shown here belong to a white-supremacist, or "skinhead," gang. Several of these gangs are affiliated with the Ku Klux Klan.

Skinheads often participate in racist events such as Ku Klux Klan marches. Members of African-American gangs often go the same marches to oppose the skinheads. Not surprisingly, violence often breaks out.

Bill Riccio, the "commander" of the National Aryan Front, explained the purpose of the rally. "We're trying to make a point here today," he said. "We designate Alabama as a white homeland." Eighteen-year-old Adam Galleon, a Confederate Hammer Skinhead who came all the way from Jacksonville, Florida, for the march, was eager to talk to reporters about it. "Hopefully, it'll be violent," he said. There was a good chance that it would be violent. Just a few months before, on April 18, a 36-year-old black man named Benny Rembert had been stabbed to death under a highway. Skinheads claimed at least partial responsibility for the murder.

Among the crowd were members of the Malcolm X Grassroots Movement, who walked next to the skinheads on the sidewalk chanting, "Hey, hey, ho, ho, racist crackers gotta go!" But their approach was mild compared to that of some members of all-black youth gangs living in Birmingham. One gang member was named "Homicidal." When he was interviewed about the march, he said about one of the Skinheads, "I want to put my ruler to his head and see the whiteness of his eyes when he dies."

"Just you wait," shouted a member of another black youth gang, called the Folks, "we're gonna get 'em!"

What was really happening in Birmingham on that day? In truth, the attitudes on both sides, white and black, were not about *race* but about *racism*. Racism requires a special kind of ignorance mixed with a special kind of rage. Anyone who has studied

DESPERATE MEASURES

Some city governments are so frustrated by the irrational killings by gang members in their neighborhoods that they have resorted to shock tactics. In 1992, the Human Relations Commission of Evanston, Illinois, authorized a TV ad campaign comparing black street gangs to Ku Klux Klansmen and neo-Nazis. The ad first showed a neo-Nazi, while a narrator stated, "If they gave a medal for killing black people, this gang would win a bronze." A message on the screen said that from 1981 to 1991, neo-Nazis had been arrested for twelve murders. The next image to appear was a hooded Klansman, while the narrator said, "This gang would win the silver." A message on the screen said that from 1960 to 1991, Klan members had been arrested for twenty known murders. Finally, a young man representing a black gang member appeared on screen, and the narrator announced, "But this gang would win the gold. If you're in a gang, you're not a brother. You're a traitor." The last message on the screen claimed that black gangs were responsible for at least 1,300 murders in 1991 alone.

The ad caused widespread complaint in Evanston because it showed only a black gang member. Officials promised that future announcements would be altered to reflect the fact that violent gang members come from every race and ethnic background.

a little history would find it impossible to stereotype any particular race or ethnic culture as all good or all bad. If you're looking for acts of injustice, cruelty, and mass stupidity, you can find them in the history books dealing with any civilization that ever existed. If you're looking for the just, the wise, or the powerful, these same civilizations produced and nurtured individuals, communities, and nations that exemplified all the virtues.

In order to hate a particular ethnicity, you've got to keep yourself from finding out too much about its people. You have to stay dumb. Otherwise your cartoon version of who they are will be threatened and destroyed.

If you want to see your own race as vastly superior, you also will have to block out a lot. You are going to have to ignore the crimes, acts of greed, or failures that every group has its share of. You are also going to have to keep running away from who you really are inside. That is because feel-

Skinheads march at a rally in Atlanta. These gang members often use patriotism as an excuse for racism and violence.

ings of superiority are often a cover-up for deep doubts about yourself. People who secretly feel powerless, inferior, or unattractive sometimes try to drown out these intolerable thoughts with edgy boasting, contempt for others, and desperate dreams of power.

Think for a moment, and you will realize that you have met these kinds of people before. They are scornful of those who are different, obsessed with others' faults. If you examine them closely you see that the criticism is really a kind of unadmitted self-criticism. It is as if these people were shouting at the mirror, hating everything they see in others that remind them of themselves.

The groups that marched that day in Birmingham had that feeling. They were pretending to be "proud and white," but inside many of them may have really felt small and humiliated. Some of them came from economically blighted areas of the South where the standard of living had sunk. Said one black woman watching from the crowd,

These people are marching against us, but they're the ones who feel like "niggers" inside. By that I mean they feel like their own stereotype of a worthless person. I hope this goose-stepping down the main street will chill 'em out a little by making 'em feel like somebody for a while.

ANGRY, WHITE, PROUD

In Chapter 2 you read about the Diamond Heights group, which started with good intentions. It was founded partly on ethnic pride. One of its values, at least at the beginning, was to increase its members' consciousness about the positive aspects of being Chicano. As you go through different situations in life, it will be your responsibility to see the difference between pride in one's background and pride based on rage and insecurity, like that shown at the Birmingham rally.

In more cases than one, gangs made up of a single ethnicity get their energy from a bitter sense of inferiority, a simmering anger about not "getting what I deserve." High school student Jimmy Schmidt, of Brentwood, California, is a typical example of that kind of motivation. His "crew" has only eleven members. But they've developed their own set of colors, their own handshake, and their own code of values. The solidarity of their crew arose around the O.J. Simpson trial. It is their fierce belief that Nicole Brown Simpson died because she was married to a black man. Jimmy sums it up like this:

> *If she had married one of her own people, she would be alive today, so I guess she got what was coming to her. On the outside he dressed like a gentleman and bought her the kind of things a decent person should have. But no matter how much he tried, he could never get rid of his negro nature which is all about being violent and full of primitive stuff.*

The ideas of Jimmy's crew are not based on any scientific fact, yet they can hold forth on them for hours, as if they came from the finest research sources. It doesn't matter how many examples of black judges, scholars, ministers, artists, or writers who enriched America you provide for Jimmy and his crew. They don't want to hear about it. It also doesn't matter if you try to connect high statistics of violence in urban black communities with the disadvantages of poverty or prejudice. According to Jimmy and his crew, black people are inherently violent because they are born with animal natures. The crew doesn't think blacks should have the same rights as whites in the United States. They look back with nostalgia to the past when prejudice against blacks was more widespread and intermarriages between different races were less common. Jimmy explains:

The purpose of our organization—well, we call it "The Return of the White Man"—it's to put things back the way they were before the Civil War. We think either blacks should leave this country or they should become slaves again. But they have no business living among white people. They just aren't going to obey the same laws.

Jimmy and his friends have a lot more to say about their philosophy, but it is so misguided and so unpleasant that you wouldn't want to read it. Listening to him talk can fill you with astonishment and make you want to know how he arrived at his absurd ideas. The answer probably lies in his own situation in society and his inability to deal with it.

Jimmy and his friends live in the posh suburb of Brentwood, where O.J. Simpson and Nicole Brown Simpson had their lavish home. However, neither Jimmy nor his crew come from families that have any money. Their crew formed in 1990 at a time when unemployment was high and most of their fathers were out of work.

Jimmy's father isn't out of work, but he works as a gardener for wealthy homeowners in Brentwood. Sometimes Jimmy has to spend his weekends as his father's assistant, hauling wheelbarrows of topsoil or raking yards. He and his friends are actually a minority in Brentwood because most of the people they live around have money.

Jimmy's mother comes from an East Coast family that came to America many generations ago and had a high standard of living and a lot of social prestige. His mother went to some of the more exclusive private schools when she was young but became rebellious in the 1960s and eloped with Jimmy's father, who came from a poorer background. Because her family objected to her marriage, they cut off their support. His mother doesn't complain about being "downwardly mobile," and doesn't seem to regret her marriage. However, on the two occasions that Jimmy has gone East, he's seen the large houses and cultivated manners of the relatives on his mother's side of the family.

It's obvious after talking to Jimmy that he is enraged at not getting what he thinks he's entitled to. He lives among people who are wealthy, and one side of his own family even lives way above the level he's used to. Instead of admitting the feeling of inferiority this has caused, it is easier for him to fix his anger on people who are different. Blaming them for his bitterness gives him a convenient target for his rage.

Of course, it would be better for Jimmy to confront his feelings and eventually come to the conclusion that having less money than the other people around him doesn't necessarily make him less of a person. It might also be good

Ethnic gangs sometimes battle each other even when they seem to have a lot in common. Considering all other gangs inferior is part of gang culture.

for him to discuss with his mother exactly why she gave up all of her financial advantages to marry his father. But Jimmy can face none of these issues squarely. It's easier to direct his rage against a fantasy image of "the black" than it is to direct it against his family.

RACE GANGS GONE HAYWIRE

So irrational is the pride of the single-ethnicity gang that it sometimes leads to the most absurd situations. In such a gang, defining who one is and how that identity is superior to all others can set people of the same race against each other. Such is the case in Hartford, Connecticut, were the Los Solidos gang often battles the Latin Kings or the Netas. These gangs are large nationwide conglomerates actively involved in crime. All three of these gangs are Latino, yet each has learned to judge the other as inferior. In late December 1994, a huge memorial meeting of Los Solidos was held at a banquet hall in Hartford to commemorate the one-year anniversary death of Felipe Santana, who was killed in a shootout by the Latin Kings.

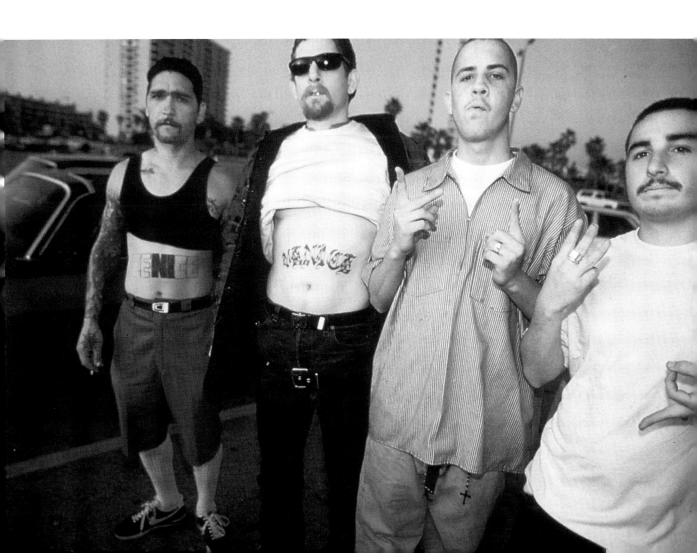

The talk whenever any of these gangs get together is about their superiority. Whether it be a question of intelligence, courage, or energy, members from each of the gangs claim that they are "the best." What is the difference between these claims and claims of racial superiority? Not much, actually, and many members of these gangs would be the first to admit it.

In New York City, a member of one of these gangs, who called himself J.R., talked about his attitude toward the members of rival Latino gangs.

> *You must be joking, bro, if you can't see the superiority of our group over the [name withheld]. They got plenty of retards, people who was born with brain problems cause their mom was drinking or taking drugs when she pregnant. But in our Nation, man, they only take the cream of the crop. We got the best of the race. I see it being our duty to stamp out those that give Latinos a bad name. If it was up to [name of his gang], our race'd be rulers of America, and not down there wasting away on the streets like so many of our people.*

In reality, J.R.'s gang has people of varying intelligence and health. It's like any other group of people. However, he hangs onto the idea of belonging to a superior group because it makes him feel better about himself. It also puts the blame for problems in the Latino community on another group, rather than the one he associates himself with. Unfortunately, this form of self-deception leads to the very opposite of the benefits of ethnic pride. It sets Latino against Latino in an endless round of misplaced anger and violence.

AVOIDING THE RACE GANG TRAP

The information in this chapter may have given you some insight into the misguided aims of the ethnic gang. The question is, how can you avoid being drawn in by such a gang's lies and promises of superiority? Remembering some of the points below could help you a great deal. You will want to think about them before you join any group of people on the basis of shared racial or cultural similarities.

Confront your prejudices. Are you angry at any particular group of people? The reasons may seem obvious to you at first. You may be able to point to the lifestyles, standard of living, crime rate, or levels of education in that group as "proof" of their inferiority. Before you do, try reading up on their history. How did they come to America? What is life in their original country like now and what was it like in the distant past? What is the history of their treatment here? What discriminatory laws in your community were once or still are geared toward them?

Once you have a real picture of who these people were and are, take a second look at your anger at them. You may find that you are angry at your own caricature of them rather than at who they really are. Now that you know that, get to know them. Make an effort to make friends with people of different cultures and ethnicities. You'll be surprised to find how much like you some of them are.

Next, take a long, hard look at your own life. Do you feel mistreated or neglected by society or community? A healthy rage about the unfairness and prejudice that has been directed against you will lead to courageous action and a strong will on your part. If you feel unhappy about the social situation of your family, think about how they got into it. Question your parents and discuss your dissatisfaction. If they're not the kind of people you can talk to, discuss the issues with an understanding friend, teacher, counselor, or member of the clergy. Find out why you are angry and how you ended up where you are. Even if there is no immediate solution to it, knowing the true story of your situation and your real feelings about it will keep you from misdirecting your anger and forming fantasy theories of superiority. Without those fantasy theories, the principles of the race gang won't hold water.

Learn about real self-respect and personal power. Throughout history, theories of racial superiority have arisen when people felt insecure and threatened, often when they were suffering from great financial hardship. If you are threatened by such conditions, desperate solutions won't get you out of them. Learning to understand that self-worth comes from within rather than from the approval of the outside world is a first step to overcoming any feelings of inferiority about being poor, not having enough education, or lacking social power.

You should be aware that lasting financial success or social power rarely come from gang membership. Gang membership may bring in money and nice clothes for a while, but it isn't the kind of secure money that can come from a high-paying job that is the result of developed work skills. Because such a way of earning money is so risky, today's fabulous car can change into tomorrow's prison cell in the blink of an eye. The same with power. You may be able to put down certain groups in the community, but there will always be one that has the power to put you down.

People who want more money and more social clout eventually learn that patience and independence are what they need. They believe in themselves regardless of what society thinks of them now. They spend their energy on training programs or school work rather than on developing an image of themselves as "gods." They've come to the conclusion that no group of any kind is going to put what they want in their lap no matter how enthusiastically they do its bidding. They've also realized that ethnic pride is about helping oneself and one's neighbors, not following leaders who tout claims of superiority and promise that they'll be ruling the world in a week

4

COLORS, CODES, AND VENDETTAS

The colors got power.
—Tito, age 17

Tito sat on the broken-down mattress on the floor in one of his gang's "cribs" in Brooklyn, New York. The cribs were abandoned apartments that his gang had claimed as hang-out places or crash pads for whoever needed to get out of the rain or cold. The walls of the crib had peeling plaster. A large hunk had fallen out of one wall, revealing the beams. There was also a hole in the floor so that you had to step carefully to make it to the mattress, or else you'd end up with one leg sticking through the ceiling of the apartment below.

Tito's appearance was in strange contrast to the broken-down apartment. His hair was perfectly close-cropped with a razor part etched into both sides. From his neck hung seven gleaming solid-gold chains. He wore a backward baseball cap over a neatly folded bandanna of his gang's colors. His Reeboks were two-toned, the same colors as his baseball cap and bandanna. On the bare shoulder revealed by his tank top were three tattooed initials, which stood for the name of the gang. Everything about his appearance was in perfect order. You had the feeling that he spent an hour getting the gold just right, the part re-etched, and the Reeboks in perfect shape before he set foot on the street. But the extreme neatness of his appearance wasn't what was most striking about him.

Gang members take great pride in wearing their colors—clothing, tattoos, jewelry, and other gear that symbolize their membership in the gang.

What anyone who saw Tito noticed first was the tattooed teardrop at the corner of one eye. If your gaze fixed upon it, it didn't embarrass him. It delighted him. He wanted to tell you what it meant. He had just turned seventeen and had spent his first six months in Rikers Island jail as a gang-related robbery suspect. Because there wasn't enough evidence, he'd finally been released. But the teardrop was there to symbolize the fact that he'd done time. When he got out, a friend drew it on his face, using a pen connected to a pencil sharpener motor. Tito said it had "made me a man."

> *The tear is going to be telling to everybody that I did time, you see. People step out of the way when they see something like that on your face. It means you down by law and they better step off. My mother when she saw it on my face says to me, "Tito, you sick? What's a matter with you?" She don't see so well so she thought it was some kind of a sore or something. I says, "Ma, I ain't sick, I'm a man now." She starts to crying and says, "What kind a man gonna mess up his face so no girl ever want to become his wife?" I told her, "Listen, Ma, you know what this does to girls? They know you're bad and they all want to be with you. They know you going to protect them on the street. They know you ain't a boy."*

Gang tattoos signify membership in the gang more permanently than clothing or jewelry. They are a symbol of commitment to the gang. The number on this man's scalp signifies his membership in the 18th Street gang in Los Angeles.

When Tito talks about being a man, he sees tattoos, clothes, and jewelry as providing the sole proof of it. How exactly can a homemade tattoo make somebody a man? When pressed for an answer, Tito says:

> *First of all, it hurts like hell, especially right there under the eye. You got to be a man to put up with it. Second of all, it stands for something. It's like if you was wearing a football insignia or something. "I stand for this. This is me. You see this, you see me." No sissy going to be wearing one of these under his eye or he going to get challenged.*

For Tito, the teardrop is a symbol of a way of life. It tells the world who he is every moment of the day: he's somebody who has been to jail and is proud of it. The teardrop is a sign that he has suffered but also wants to boast about it. Anyone who would wear it is not the kind of person who is satisfied with letting people discover who he is. He wants his image of himself shouted at the world.

When Tito talks about his "colors," his eyes burn with excitement. Every careful costume he puts together incorporates the two colors of his gang. He was eager to explain what the colors symbolized. One supposedly stood for total obedience to the laws and lords of the gang. It was supposed to be a reminder that the only way to break allegiance to those laws was by death. The other color was supposed to symbolize pride. Pride wasn't based on what the gang or the individual had accomplished. It was based purely on the fact of wearing that particular color! As Tito put it:

> *You see anybody puts on these colors gets strong from them almost like by magic. The colors got power. They hook you up to every other G that puts that stuff on. You know what I'm saying? It don't matter if you afraid to walk down the street. Put on the colors and—pow!—you got a nation backing you up. The colors is strength!*

As Tito talked, the more it became obvious that he thought of his body as a blank page to illustrate. The tattoo, gang colors, and expensive gold showed who he was supposed to be on this body. For almost an hour he told the story of each gold chain. He wanted to tell what act of violence or friendship he had performed to win each chain. His stories were like legends, told in a way to portray himself as fearless or generous or as faithful and loyal to his nation. The "kicks," or sneakers, Tito wore were also a symbol of his gang solidarity. But their high price was also something he wanted to associate with himself. As he saw it, clothes made the man. All you had to do was put on a certain image and you became it.

Clothes have always been an intimate expression of personality and taste. People sometimes express who they are by wearing them. Clothes are also a symbol of your affiliation with a particular group. That's why lawyers tend to wear the same style of suits or members of the same sorority often are attracted to similar fashions.

For gang members, clothes have become a uniform. How do uniforms differ from civilian clothes? They are a much stricter expression of affiliation with a group. They are a sign that the person wearing them is subject to specific rules and allegiances. A person who wears a uniform puts more emphasis on thinking according to group guidelines than on thinking as an individual. In the case of a uniform, the clothes do "make the man."

For Tito, his tattoos and clothing were almost fetishes. A fetish is an object thought by some cultures to have magical powers. It may be a bone belonging to some sacred animal, a stone, or a carving. Fetishes were used in ceremonies to evoke spirits, or carried or worn to keep away evil. Tito actually thought that just wearing his colors made him powerful. He thought that wearing expensive chains meant that he himself was of great value as well.

People with a strong desire to belong often resort to outward symbols of allegiance. Wearing a baseball cap with the name of your favorite team seems to link you to their glory and their success. It can make you feel special. Gang members often need the uniform of gangs to get through life. Without these props they feel empty or vulnerable. Who are they if they are not a member of

Tattoos, gold jewelry, and the right "look" give gang members a sense of belonging and pride.

their nation? They may feel cut off from their family and their culture. They may feel alone and at risk. Gang colors are like an instant new flag and a new country. Expensive jewelry, a new leather coat, or fashionable kicks pump up your ego and make you a part of their mystique.

A LIFE FOR A "LOOK"

At Aleysha J.'s high school in the Bronx, you won't get anywhere unless you have a certain look. Huge gold earrings, designer clothes, and leather separate the girls who are "in" from those who are "out." It's hard to tell one girl from another as they file out of the school at day's end. All seem to have the same pulled-back hair style, dark red lipstick, and earrings shaped like door knockers.

Aleysha made *The New York Times* in 1991 in a story about high school girls and crime. The number of girls involved in violent crime had been increasing regularly in the past four years, and the *Times* wanted to find out why. They found that a lot of the girls were getting into trouble merely to keep up their expensive "look."

"It's like I don't want to do it," Aleysha told a reporter, "but my friends put a lot of pressure on me. Then I see something I want so bad I just take it. The worst time, I pulled a knife on this girl, but I never hurt anybody. I just want things."

Aleysha may not have hurt anybody, but other girls with the same needs and desires have. Shortly before the *Times* article was written, a girl named Maribel Feliciano was attacked on the subway by a pack of girls who wanted her hoop earrings. She died, and four of the girls now face murder charges.

Symbols of power and riches take on great importance when people feel they have neither. The confident person does not feel he or she has anything to prove with clothing. Such a person simply wears what he or she likes with the goal of expressing feelings and attitudes and putting together a pleasing outfit. That person's taste may be flashy or conservative. He or she may like looks that blend in and work anywhere or looks that always stand out and make a statement. It all depends on individual personality.

There is no strict dividing line between those who dress for pleasure and self-expression, as described in the paragraph above, and those who desperately strive for an image, as both Tito and Aleysha do. However, the more clothes resemble a uniform, the more one has given up individual feelings and ideas in favor of the group. Why would anybody want to do this? The answer lies in the fact that latching on to a ready-made system of values and goals can be very attractive. It's easier than thinking for yourself.

You yourself may be very interested in your appearance. There is nothing wrong with that. But how much of your appearance is a reflection of who you

Heavy gold earrings, pulled-back hair, designer clothes, and bright red lipstick are common "looks" for girls associated with gangs.

really are? And how much of it is an expression of a need to belong? Do you feel like yourself when you put your clothes on? Would you still dress that way if nobody else did? Who would approve of the way you dress? Is that the reason for your choice of clothing? Who would disapprove of it? Is that why you wear the clothes you do?

Gangs prescribe colors and looks for their members because they wish to discourage individual thought. A gang is like an army. People who dress the same are agreeing to live by the same code. Each day they rise and clothe themselves in the values of the gang. If they feel they have nothing without the gang, putting on the gang's colors can produce a thrilling feeling of being whole.

In reality, the colors are nothing but a symbol. Although they produce a feeling of power, there is no real power in them. You can be courageous, loyal, alert, or generous in a potato sack. You can be cowardly, sneaky, unaware, and selfish in the spiffiest kicks or the most impressive tattoo. The danger in the heavy emphasis on a "look" promoted by gangs is that it distracts people from working to forge real identities. It lulls them into thinking that they can magically become who they want to be by putting on the right clothes.

CODES OF BEHAVIOR

Gangs also rely on codes of behavior to squelch individual thought and to control members. Codes of behavior have always been a part of most occupations and organizations. When a person becomes a doctor, he or she takes the Hippocratic oath, vowing to uphold certain moral and professional principles. All religions have prescribed codes of behavior that believers are supposed to follow.

In gangs, codes of behavior work the same as colors and clothing. They ensure that each member will act as a cog in the wheel of the larger machine and maintain its smooth functioning. Gangs are often run like police states. No deviations from the rules are allowed. Those who do deviate will be harshly punished. Below are some principles of the code of Los Solidos, the Latino gang on the East Coast that you read about earlier:

- The gang's charter is the "bible." It is written down, and the pages must be handled carefully. No one is allowed to touch it with dirty hands.
- Once you become a member, there is no way out. You cannot quit.
- You must always wear your red and blue colors and have a tattoo representing the gang. It can be a logo, a skull, or the letters "L.S.N."
- If you get arrested, reveal nothing. There is nothing more detestable than a "snitch."
- Members must show respect for one another. Jailed members get visits, mail, money, and clothing.
- If a member dies, all other members must attend the funeral.
- Each meeting starts with a prayer asking God to "bless the family."

At first look, the code of behavior of Los Solidas makes it seem almost like a strict religious order. However, the Los Solidos code takes on a stranger

GUNS ARE ROMANTIC

A recent newspaper article discussed the romance of guns for teenagers in the city of Omaha, Nebraska. The guns are a symbol of status, and a teenager who only owns a .22-caliber pistol is considered to be less "cool" than one who owns a .357 Magnum. According to the article, protection or even criminal activity are not the motives of many teenagers who get guns. The main motive is status.

Offering further proof of the romance of guns for kids was the 5-year-old boy in Camp Springs, Maryland, who in 1995 brought a loaded semiautomatic to school for show-and-tell.

The popularity of guns and the status they confer has become a national problem. Guns cause one out of every four deaths among American teenagers. In 1990, 4,200 teenagers were killed by guns.

Gangs punish members who do not follow a strict code of behavior. Here two gang members give a third member a "violation," or beating, for committing an offense against the gang code.

aspect when you realize that one of the main objectives of the group is drug dealing. There are more codes about "the business" that prescribe how to handle the drugs, when not to talk about them, and how to carry out the various roles necessary to distribute them. In light of this, all the supportive, respectful behavior seems focused on a negative goal.

The "religious" feeling of the Los Solidos codes point to its members' deep need for guidance and for something to believe in. Many of them come from homes without fathers. No one cares about the hours they keep, what they eat, or where they go. The majority have dropped out of school. They have no other discipline but the code of Los Solidos. It structures their day for them and gives them something to believe in. So strict is the code that the members are like knights with a divine purpose. They feel no need to question their values or feelings, but only to follow orders.

Members of a gang follow codes for the sake of having something to follow. Thinking that you know what you believe in and doing what is "right" every day can give you a blissful sense of security. It can keep you from independently questioning right from wrong. Unfortunately, such strict observance is often attached to activities that involve drugs and violence. But gang members who follow codes get comfort and pleasure from being obedient, so it is unlikely that they will question the reasons for a rule.

THE MYSTIQUE OF SPORTS

In the mid-1990s, inner-city people from San Diego to Baltimore began sporting Los Angeles Raiders jackets, hats, and other clothing with the official insignia of the team, and officials are worried. They suspect that for many youths, the Raiders clothing has become a ready-made gang uniform. Apparently, the Crips, an enormous complex of gangs centered in Los Angeles, started wearing the caps around the same time that they expanded their drug operations around the country.

Some say that people associated with gangs prefer the Raiders clothing (and other sports insignia and clothing) because of the ready-made tough image that comes with it. Georgetown University's insignia is popular because the school is famous for its college basketball team and because G can also stand for gangster. But others think the style is a cover-up, an attempt to look normal while engaged in illegal activity. "You can hide behind what is seen as good," said Betty J. Germany, a school administrator who helped ban Raiders gear from all high schools in Denver. "I think they simply used it as a kind of cover."

The connection between sports gear and gangs raises some important issues. At what point does good, "clean" aggression become destructive? How can a society produce some of the world's most famous athletes and some of the world's most ferocious gang leaders? It shows how gangs can take over the ordinary competitive spirit that has always been part of America and use it to their own ends.

Whatever the reason for the popularity of Raiders gear, it seems obvious that gang members would identify with the world of sports. Team playing is important to the survival of a gang. Individual differences have to be overcome if the gang is to operate effectively. The same holds for sports. What is more, like sports, gang life is about the competition of one group against another.

Of course, sports are a leisure-time activity. The competition is for fun and it is hoped that no one will be seriously hurt. Gang competition is "for keeps." It involves serious hurt and a ruthless intention for gain.

You are probably familiar with moments in sports history when sports got "out of hand." Whether it was a town ruined by rioting after a football game, or one skater arranging for another to be injured, the dark side of sports competition was apparent. It will be up to you to evaluate competitiveness with eyes

Gear representing the Raiders football team is popular among gang members because the team has a reputation for being aggressive and tough.

wide open. How important is it to win? Is it worth hurting others? Is being a team player on a soccer team any different than using the same team-playing skills to sell drugs? Which is more important, winning or why you strive to win?

VENDETTAS

An inevitable part of the codes of most gangs is the code of the vendetta. Vendetta means "vengeance" in Italian. It is often a long feud, marked by many bloody incidents. When it comes to the vendetta, the system of codes of most gangs falls apart. According to the codes of most gangs, a vendetta is supposed to right a wrong. It is "paying back" a rival gang or enemy for a hurt done.

But is a vendetta a paying back of another vendetta? The trail of violence leading back from most gang feuds is so long that it is usually impossible to tell "who started it first." A hurt inflicted on one gang by another is usually a vendetta for past wrongs, real or imagined. Then it is the other gang's turn to strike back. The cycle goes on endlessly. More and more lives are lost. The stakes of the vendetta become higher and higher. Rage grows. Vows keep being made. All involved think they are right. The killing never stops.

Why doesn't someone step aside and say, "Wait a minute. There is no end to this. If I strike out at you, eventually you will get me back." No one asks this in a gang until things are way out of control because the vendetta has ceased to be a way of accomplishing anything. It is just a "feeling." In many gangs, a vendetta is just a belief about correct behavior. It's totally impractical. "If your brother is hurt, you must hurt back," pure and simple. No one thinks about what is in store down the road. Participating in a vendetta is like putting on colors. It is a ritual. When gang members carry out a vendetta together, they feel close to each other. It is a ceremony of togetherness that usually accomplishes little and points the way to more violence.

James B., a Los Angeles high school student who has dropped out of gangs but who used to participate in vendettas, explained it like this:

> I talked this over with my counselor for a long time. Why would I go on raids to rough other guys up, sometimes even cripple them, for the slightest wrong? I knew they'd be back next week with their own group to get us. I knew we weren't getting anywhere. But you see, it wasn't about getting anywhere. It was kind of like a statement. It was like saying nobody messes with us. You weren't saying it alone, but with a whole bunch of people saying it together. It's kind of like at a football game when you all cheer together about creaming the other team. You do it out of togetherness. You do it to feel strong, I guess.

Vendettas getting out of hand are what got James B. out of gang life. However, it took a pretty dangerous incident to break the cycle of vendettas he was caught in.

> I would go to school on Monday and this rival crew would pounce on us. I'm white, you know, but it wasn't about that. Both the gangs were mixed—blacks, white, Chicano. No, it was just about who your friends were. Then who you hanged with froze up into a gang when other people started picking on you. Or at least that's what it seemed like. So on Monday a rival crew would pounce on us. On Wednesday we'd get them back, and on Friday they'd get us again. At first it was just scrapes and a couple of broken wrists. But they started happening more and more often. The kids who weren't hooked up with a crew started forming their own because they were getting paranoid about the violence. Anyway, one day somebody threw a blade into the mix, for the first time. A kid got wounded pretty badly. I came home to my parents and said, "I don't want any more of this." So they yanked me out of school and put me in another one.

James was luckier than a lot of people who get involved with gangs because his parents were there for him. He'd tried to keep what was happening at school from them, but they'd become suspicious when he came home bruised or with his clothing torn. As soon as he spoke up, they took immediate action. A student who couldn't talk to his parents might still be at the same school, caught in the vendetta cycle.

If you are one of those students who can't talk to your parents, think about your options. What would happen if you refused to participate in the vendetta cycle? Would you become the next target of it? If so, is there a counselor, a teacher, or a law officer whom you can trust? But it must be a person who realizes the dangers of intervention when it comes to gang vendettas. Someone who has no understanding of the situation you are in could do more harm than good. There are, however, counselors, therapists, and law officers who specialize in the culture of gangs. Such a person might be just the one you need to speak to.

THE HIGH PRICE OF MACHISMO

Aleysha J., whom you read about earlier in this chapter, is part of a growing trend of violence among teenage girls and young women. The statistics on female violence have been rising yearly. However, gang violence and violence in general is still mostly male. Why is this so?

A lot of this has to do with the active role assigned males in our society. Men are expected to remain in control and hide their emotions more than women are. The high end of this attitude, in which males are defined by very narrow codes of stoic and aggressive masculinity, is called *machismo*, from a Spanish word meaning "maleness."

Many Latino cultures stress machismo as a positive value. From the time a boy is a toddler, the older males in his family and community encourage him to walk, talk, think, and feel like a "real man." However, Latino cultures are far from having the patent on this attitude. All cultures have it in some degree. Some would argue that it even started with a biological basis. They cite studies hinting that testosterone, a male hormone, can cause aggressive behavior. Whether this is true or not remains to be seen. It is also obvious that certain cultures depend on the values of machismo to keep their communities functioning smoothly. It is not the purpose of this book to discuss machismo as a value in itself. However, the destructive behavior of many gangs stems from *exaggerated* attitudes of machismo. These attitudes reveal a secret insecurity about "being a man." To counteract the insecurity, they constantly attempt to prove their machismo.

Exaggerated machismo often comes into play during the teenage years when boys becoming men are still uncertain of their strengths and capabilities. The frozen-hipped swagger that they may then affect looks more like playing at being men than the way grown men actually walk. You'll find the same swagger

Vendettas start when a gang retaliates against another a gang, starting a cycle of violence that is hard to break. The victims are sometimes gang members—and sometimes innocent bystanders caught in the crossfire.

among many male gang members as they seek to prove to the world beyond a shadow of a doubt that they are strong and brave and "manly."

The values of machismo take some males a long way in the world and sustain them against misfortune, the challenges of others, and feelings that might overcome them. However, when machismo gets too rigid, it becomes a disadvantage. For example, standing up to pressure is a useful strength that can get you through difficult situations. But when the "pressure" is made up of people pointing out your mistakes or how you are wrong, macho strength can become stubborn pig-headedness. Mature men have been known to admit when they are wrong.

People who value machismo often express distaste for displays of weakness. A male who cries in public or shows an unwillingness to face danger is met with scorn. The attitude works in situations of extreme emergency, where anything that delays action can endanger the entire group. The battlefield is a good example. However, scorn for weakness or expressions of suffering outside of emergency situations shows a lack of compassion. It also forces the scornful one to bottle up his emotions and hide them from others no matter how great the pain. Since the emotions have to go somewhere, they often remain in a secret place, eating away at the personality. They keep a person from living fully and from loving others. The emotions are still there, but they find other, twisted ways to express themselves, such as in acts of anger.

The acting-out of anger is usually applauded by those who value machismo highly. Strangely enough, this one particular expression of emotion is allowed. Since it is the only emotion allowed to be expressed publicly, it often takes the place of other negative feelings. Thus, someone who feels horrible about his mother being ill might express it by getting into a violent fight on a weak pretext. Letting out the pain this way disguises it with a show of strength and may win the applause of other macho peers.

STAYING "REAL"

In a sense the theme of this chapter has been about not staying true to oneself. It's about borrowing identity and direction from a group instead of forging it on one's own. The colors, codes, and vendettas of gang life are a brave imitation of character, power, values, feelings, and personality, but they are mostly a disguise. Although they are hooked up to real elements of a person's personality, they promise more than might be there, and are not wholly "real" kinds of behavior. Nevertheless, colors, codes, and vendettas can exert a great appeal.

How can you avoid the lure of easy answers when it comes to trying to be a "real" person? How can you express who you are, find something to believe in, and grow comfortable with your feelings without relying too much on clothing, strict behavior codes, or violent behavior? It might help to keep in mind some of the following points.

Clothes don't make the person. Keep in mind that clothes *show* who you are, but they don't *make* who you are. No amount of expensive gear can fill up what you think you lack. Hard work leading toward school or career success and sharing fears and insecurities with good friends are both real ego-boosters. Colors and logos symbolize beliefs and attitudes you like, but they don't automatically make those beliefs or attitudes successful. If you are a flashy dresser, decide to use the "flash" fearlessly. Show people who you really are without worrying about which category it puts you in. If you aren't flashy, and would rather "fit in," that's fine, too. But question the values of what you want to "fit in" with. Make sure it's in line with what you truly believe.

Consider the means, not just the end. Aleysha J. got a charge out of big hoop earrings and designer clothes. Sometimes her need for them led her to do things she wished she hadn't done. When you go for something you want, find a way to get it that you won't regret later.

Find your own codes. If life were a fill-in-the-blanks business, you could just fill in the spaces and sit back and watch it take shape. But that's not why you have brains. Codes of honor, loyalty, and courage are examples of good behavior, but they always need to be questioned. Think for yourself. Question any group that has a strict code of rules. Don't always go with the "party line."

Keep your competitive spirit healthy. In this country, competition is a force in school, business, and sports. It sharpens skills and gives people the motivation to succeed. But like any good thing, it can become a bad habit. Winning for the sake of winning only works in sports. In the rest of life it can be foolish or destructive. Compete for fun or to get what you want, not just for the sake of being right or being powerful.

Learn about justice. Don't get caught in the cycle of vengeance. Know in advance that there will be no end to it. If someone is doing you a wrong, act to stop it as soon as possible. Once a wrong is already done, "getting back" won't do you any tangible good. Protecting yourself means taking measures to end violence quickly. It may mean a pow-wow with the offending party. It may mean involving the police or a concerned adult. Think enough of yourself to settle a dispute with the potential for the least harm to you, now and in the future.

Redefine manhood. If you're macho, sort through the codes of behavior you live by. Which macho attitudes are a benefit to you and those you care about? Which keep getting you into trouble? Learn that being a man also means admitting your mistakes. Get rid of habits that get you into trouble. Work on those manly qualities that let you express all your feelings in a dynamic way. Find someone who won't judge you for expressing vulnerable feelings and confide in that person regularly.

Gangs tell you who to hang out with, how you should dress, and what you should think—but you don't need a gang to form your own identity.

5
GANGS ARE BIG BUSINESS

These people weren't really looking out for me.
They were using me.
—T. Love, age 19

They call him Hong Kong Boy. He's a 20-year-old science major at a college in Queens, New York City. Starting at seven every evening, however, you won't find him on the college campus. That is when he begins his patrol of Mott Street, in Manhattan's Chinatown. He carries a .357 Magnum and keeps an eye open for the members of rival gangs. On one arm is an eagle and a skull. This emblem identifies him as a member of the Chinese Ghost Shadow gang.

To Hong Kong Boy, who was born in this country but spent some time in Hong Kong, the Ghost Shadows are the meaning of life itself. Almost everything he does is planned by his leader, or Dai Lo, which means "elder brother." The Dai Lo pays his college tuition, tells him what gang business to take care of, and supplies him with all the money he needs. In return, Hong Kong Boy patrols the streets evenings, offering protection from other gangs to the store owners, for money. Those who do not pay may be subjected to violence.

For Hong Kong Boy, the Dai Lo and his gang fill a gap left by an absent family. He admits that it isn't really money that drove him into joining a gang. It's partly the fact that he has had little contact with his mother or father for almost eight years. Hong Kong Boy's situation matches that of many of the

Many gangs are deeply involved in the business of illegal drugs—and drugs and violence go hand-in-hand.

members of the Ghost Shadows. Some come from broken homes. Others have immigrant parents struggling with several jobs at once to survive. The gang is a substitute family.

The sense of family provided by the Ghost Shadows is an intense one. Members spend almost all their time together. They eat together, see movies together, and help each other out when they are in trouble. The Dai Lo looks after most of their needs, including their clothing. The Ghost Shadows is in many ways a real family.

Support groups for Chinese immigrants are not a recent phenomenon in America. Like almost every other immigrant group, the Chinese have created their own associations. They have developed social and business organizations and various helping services designed to provide a sense of familiarity in their adopted country. During the first large wave of Chinese immigrants to the United States in the nineteenth century, many Chinese formed clubs called "tongs," which means "meeting halls." The tradition of the tongs went all the way back to the late seventeenth century in China, where similar groups, often secret, were formed to resist invading rulers. In America the tongs were and are merchants' associations that offered credit unions and business advice. Eventually, some also developed illegal gambling operations within the Chinese-American community. Today, the tongs still provide services for new immigrants, run credit unions, and fund social services in the community. But like many institutions, whether they be unions, social clubs, or political parties, some of the tongs have become corrupted. Over the years they have added gambling, protection rackets, prostitution, and drug dealing to their list of activities.

Those members of the tongs who became corrupted eventually realized they needed muscle to accomplish their goals. They began appealing to the Chinese-American youth gangs. Youth gangs had formed among young people in Chinatown for much the same reasons as gangs and cliques form among other groups. The corrupt tongs saw how valuable the members of the youth gangs could be as drug runners, shakedown artists, or bodyguards, so they started offering various gangs money, protection, and influence. The money offered the gangs was gained by extortion of honest merchants in the community or from the sale of drugs. The protection included highly paid lawyers and big-brother advisors. The influence included such benefits as being able to eat in restaurants without paying, tell younger gang members what to do, or intimidate the families of rival gangs. The alliance between corrupt tongs and gang members looking for a sense of family had become something very much unlike a family. It had become big business.

With the muscle of the tongs behind them, some youth gangs in Chinatown have begun to recruit new members forcibly. They offer protection to high school students and explain what will happen to them if they choose to remain independent. Many of these students are already the victims of gang vio-

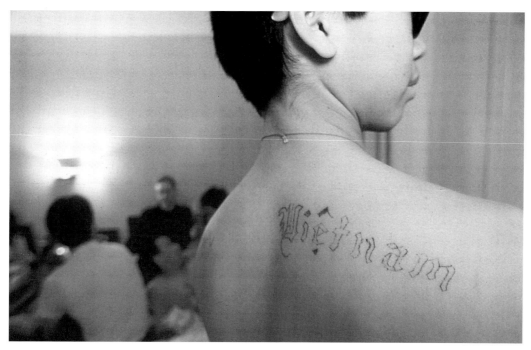

In recent years Asian gangs have become big players in the drug business. This young man is a member of a Vietnamese gang.

lence and are afraid to say no. Hong Kong Boy is such an example. A few years ago his foster sisters were raped by members of a gang. Then he was beaten up and a gun was put to his head. Later, a member of the Ghost Shadows approached him and asked him if he needed protection. That is how he became one of their members.

EXECUTIVES OF CRIME

Hong Kong Boy has plenty of money for movies and clothes. He doesn't have to worry about scraping together tuition for college. Many of his friends drive fancy cars. But who is really benefiting from the money that he helps bring in?

In the early 1990s a raid in New York City by the federal Drug Enforcement Administration uncovered a heroin ring hiding $8.6 million in cash. In another recent raid, federal agents arrested 130 people smuggling heroin from Burma, from whom they seized 200 pounds of heroin. They uncovered drug-related assets totaling $25 million. About $15 million of it was in cash, but the rest of it included Florida condos, apartment buildings, boats, and restaurants.

In Chicago twenty-nine people, including some civic leaders of New York's Chinatown, were recently indicted for operating an illegal gambling ring that had spread throughout the entire nation and brought in millions. Police have also busted several operations that smuggle Asian immigrants into the country and then imprison them and take payments from them until they have paid out $30,000. Sometimes they torture them if the payment process takes too long.

In the face of these millions in illegal earnings, the cost of free meals, fancy cars, and college tuitions for gang members like Hong Kong Boy are a drop in the bucket. The life-threatening dangers gang members face means that they may be killed at any time. That is for keeps. Is their tiny share of the profits really worth the risk? What is more, all the positive family values between gang members and their Dai Lo evaporate in the face of the disruption they are causing to the rest of the community. Since the gangs began operating, shootings are a staple of life in Chinatown. Merchants live in constant fear as the balance of power between different gangs shifts and the merchants are bullied first by one and then the other gang. Inside and outside the Chinese-American community, addiction to heroin is being promoted by the gangs and corrupt tong members who deal the drug.

A lot of young people who get involved with gangs do so without paying much attention to what is happening at the top. Suddenly they find themselves caught in a network of

A FLOATING CORPORATION

Most money-making gangs stake out territory and establish a power base. Once they have gained a strong foothold in an area, they try to expand. However, in the early 1990s some Vietnamese gangs in America established a new way of doing criminal business based on the old American model of the traveling salesman. In small groups, gang members travel from town to town, with weapons in their trunks, staking out immigrant neighborhoods. They invade the homes of immigrants, spending a few hours intimidating families with violence until the frightened people turn over their savings. In some communities hard hit by this activity, such as San Jose, California, there can be as many as forty invasions in one thirty-day period. The refugee families often make good targets because they are more likely to keep their savings and jewelry in their homes, rather than in a bank.

Public commentators see this new form of gang business as the most alienated yet. Most of the gang members come from families whose lives were torn apart by the Vietnam War. They identity neither with Vietnamese nor Americans. They can't even tolerate the "family" atmosphere of the gang with a fixed neighborhood but prefer to keep moving.

powerful criminal forces. They lose their freedom of choice and become the slaves of exploitive bosses. As the years progress, gangs like the Ghost Shadows may even find themselves being taken over by international criminal organizations. The Triad societies of Hong Kong, a powerful organization of gangsters, are working to establish themselves in New York by 1997, when Hong Kong ceases to be a British colony and becomes a part of China. Gangs like the Ghost Shadows may not have much choice as the Triad societies become established. Local gangs will be forced to serve the ends of the societies. What started as control of a couple of blocks in Chinatown will expand into the activities of an international criminal organization.

CRACK TAKES OVER

In the mid 1980s, an inexpensive way to freebase, or purify, cocaine was developed on the streets of many cities. All that it required was cocaine, baking soda, water, and a lighter. The purification process produced tiny white rocks of smokable cocaine that produced a sudden, jolting high. Freebasing this way made the crack cheap, about $3 to $5 a "rock." The high that crack produces is overwhelming and quick. After a few moments, the user craves more, in order to keep from "coming down," which could be an uncomfortable, even frightening experience. Crack is psychologically addictive. A regular user will do almost anything to stay high.

Crack permanently changed the cocaine trade. Until this time, quarter, half, and whole grams of powdered, sniffable cocaine cost from $20 to $100. It was a drug associated with the rich. It was used by people who had expendable income. But almost anyone could afford to try a rock or two of crack. Crack started catching on in poor urban neighborhoods.

As crack became a growth industry throughout the nation, gangs looking for a cheap, fast way to make money took control of its sale and distribution. Crack dealing required a lot of street-corner dealers selling small amounts of crack at a rapid rate. Gangs strove to control whole counties. Control of one central spot would not have been enough, because crack was "nicklin' and dimin'" it. At only $3 to $5 a "hit," entire neighborhoods had to be turned into crack supermarkets if the gangs were to make a big profit.

Gang involvement in the selling of crack took on two modes of operation. In the first mode, gang members sold crack but were pledged not to take it themselves. For example, the charter of the Los Solidos gang specified that members could never "use the product." Drug abuse was not allowed. Such gangs tried to create highly efficient operations. They patterned them on the standards of big businesses. The second mode of crack selling by gang members involved those who were addicted to the drug and sold it to get more of it. These operations were less predictable since workers were high while on the job. Businesses run by drug users ran less smoothly and had less clout than the more organized operations that enforced drug-free employee behavior.

When crack cocaine became popular, gangs realized that selling the drug was a quick and easy way to make money.

However, whether crack was being sold by gang members who were "clean" or who "smoked" soon became unimportant. Crack needed large sections of neighborhoods in order to be profitable. Control of the crack trade increased battles over turf and led to more frequent drive-by shootings. Many drive-by shootings became attempts to drive the dealers of one affiliation off the block by those who wanted their drug turf. Of course, thousands of innocent people were put in danger or killed by the spray of bullets that resulted. But why should the drug lords have cared? They were poisoning their own community with a highly addictive, sometimes deadly substance. It isn't surprising that they weren't concerned about who got hurt, no matter what the circumstance.

How crack ate away at entire neighborhoods has been well-documented on TV and in the newspapers. Crack-addicted parents stopped caring for their children. Young women and men became prostitutes to get the money to buy the drug. Crack addicts sometimes went on "missions" to get more of the drug, hurting anyone who stood in their way and robbing local stores or service stations.

What is less known is what happened to the small-time crack dealers. Lured by the quick money of dealing crack, they soon found themselves up to their necks in problems. They became associated with unpleasant "bosses" who were less fair, more brutal, and more greedy than the bosses of the hardest, lowest-paying legitimate jobs.

A PAWN OF THE DRUG TRADE

Jimmy S. grew up in a poor neighborhood of Boston. In 1987, his mother died of liver poisoning due to alcoholism. Jimmy's father, who had been a violent drunk, had died from the same disease ten years earlier. For that reason, Jimmy had a distaste for alcohol and drugs and vowed never to try them.

When his mother died, Jimmy went to live with an uncle who was also a heavy drinker. Jimmy's uncle didn't get violent when he drank the way his father had. He did get sentimental and childish, though. He would spend the evenings wailing about the loss of his sister, who was Jimmy's mother. Then he'd bemoan that fact that he was still slaving in a factory at the age of 52. He'd expected better things out of life, he continually told Jimmy after a few drinks. It was obvious to Jimmy, but not to his uncle, that it was alcohol that was holding his uncle back, just as it had been alcohol that had killed his mother.

Jimmy's depression about the death of his mother and his contempt for his uncle's drinking were so stressful that he eventually couldn't concentrate on schoolwork. That same year, at the age of 16, he dropped out of school. His uncle got him a job at minimum wage breaking boxes in a factory. The work was brutal and unrewarding. To take his mind off it, Jimmy began spending his evenings in

Crack destroys communities when gangs take over buildings and battle rival gangs over territory. Drug raids by the police can often lead to boarded-up buildings and ruined neighborhoods.

Boston's "Combat Zone." This is an area of Boston where pornography and prostitution abound.

When Jimmy found out about crack, he had no desire to try it. The memories of his relatives' substance abuse were too fresh in his mind. What he wanted to do almost immediately, however, was sell it. He had met dealers who said they were making $500 a night. To a person breaking his back at factory work for $40 a day, this amount seemed miraculously immense. Jimmy describes the beginning of his dealing career as follows:

> *I just took my check from work and cashed it and bought four jumbo bottles off this dealer and then rearranged the rocks inside so that each one was going to have a little bit less. I was able to make six bottles out of that and I made twenty dollars—in a half hour! I was hooked. After about a week of that I made a connection that said if I could get together a hundred dollars he could sell me enough to make a bundle. A bundle is twenty-five bottles of crack at ten dollars each, so the profit is a hundred fifty dollars.*

Everything went fine for a while. After a month, Jimmy had enough to get new sneakers and leather boots. He bought them and put them away "for a time when I wouldn't have to waste them on the street, wearing them in front of trash." At this point Jimmy didn't consider himself a real part of crack culture. He felt above it, and figured he was just taking advantage of it for a little while.

One night, however, as he was standing on the corner he had staked out for himself,

> . . . along comes this Toyota and there is a gun barrel sticking out of the window on the shotgun side. It's pointed at me. They didn't fire it, just slowed down until it was staring me in the face and after I turned white they burn rubber and they're gone. You never saw guns in the Combat Zone.
>
> The next thing I know, the next day, this dude wearing a lot of fancy leather comes up to me, slaps me on the back like I'm a friend, "Yo, you are wasting your time, bro, selling that shit like that. Now I can get you jumbos at two dollars a throw if you can buy a hundred of them but you got to package them yourself. What say?"
>
> Well, I went with him to see what it's all about and he takes me to, like, a mansion, on the hill, and inside it are all these dudes with guns and a whole cooking operation—to cook up the crack. "O.K.," I said to him, "I want in." "Well, don't you know who we are?" says the dude with the leather. "We're the [name withheld] gang and you been step-ping on our trade. If you want to keep dealing you got to get beat in [join the gang]. If you don't, you got to stop dealing or you got to kiss this." He lifts a gun and sticks it against my mouth.
>
> So I said, "Sure, sure, beat me in." I thought they were going to, you know, beat me up to make me a member, like some gangs do, but instead they made me sign an oath of loyalty that I was working for them and only them.

Jimmy's new employer started out "sweet" but soon turned sour. At the beginning, they gave him the crack at $2 a bottle. What they had neglected to mention was that after he sold the jumbo bottles for $10, he was supposed to bring them back another $6 a bottle, making his profit only $2 a bottle.

> I wasn't going to say, like, "Yo, you been playing [cheating] me," 'cause that would be disrespectful and they had talked a lot about G's that were disrespectful and what would happen to them. So they got over on me royally, but that wasn't the end of it. I come back one time and they wanted all the money I made. They wouldn't even let me keep the two dollars per bottle. The same one in leather says, "You got to be patient, we need that money 'cause we are expanding our operation. We even gonna hit the suburbs. And for every new dollar we make, you gonna get

part of it. So hold your horses. This is gonna pay off."

Jimmy was caught in the crack trade for over a year. The money he'd forfeited was never returned to him, and the same situation was repeated with every two or three transactions. Instead of the individual entrepreneur he'd planned on being, he was a lackey. The gang also used him to run dangerous errands into other neighborhoods, picking up powdered cocaine for cooking or delivering large sums of money. More than once he thought of running off with the "stash" or the money, but then he thought what would happen when they found him.

Finally, more than a year later, both the gang leader and the "dude in leather" were arrested. A struggle for control of the gang took place, and operations fell apart. Jimmy took advantage of the confusion to slip away quietly. But he knew it would be dangerous to remain in Boston. He moved to New York and got on welfare. Then he got training as a nurse's aide.

Another nurse's aide at the hospital was attracted to Jimmy. Once they were involved, she took him to Alanon, a self-help group for the family members of alcoholics. It turned out that her father had also been an alcoholic and she'd been attending Alanon for four years. Jimmy got in touch with his feelings about his family's alcoholism. His relationship with the nurse eventually ended, however.

THE FACTS ON CRACK

What are the consequences to the individual or community that has contact with crack? Once crack enters the bloodstream and reaches the brain, it stimulates the brain to release certain chemicals associated with pleasure. It also raises heartbeat and blood pressure to abnormal levels. This is why a few people have died instantly from crack. They died from sudden heart attacks or aneurysms.

Cocaine sniffed in powder form takes several minutes to reach the brain and begin having an effect upon it. Injected cocaine reaches the brain in ninety seconds. All of the cocaine in one inhale of crack reaches the brain in just seven seconds.

Cocaine and crack wear out the nerve pathways of the brain so that a habitual user finds it difficult to experience pleasure without it. Crack also eats away lung tissue and damages the heart by enlarging one particular part of its muscle tissue. Crack is partly responsible for the spread of AIDS. It can act as an aphrodisiac, and people under its influence may have multiple partners without using protection.

Crack also harms the fetuses of pregnant women. It causes low birth weight. There is evidence tying it to birth defects of every organ system. One year after it hit the streets, incidences of infant mortality and low birth weight began to rise, and they have been rising every year since.

Gang business is unpredictable and risky. It's usually only a matter of time before a gang member gets arrested.

Although he looks forward to a relationship with someone in the future, he feels he has to work through his anger before he can relate intimately on a day-to-day basis with someone.

Let's take a close look at Jimmy's psychology to see exactly why he let himself become a pawn of the drug trade. When he was questioned about how it felt to sell a dangerous, addictive drug to people suffering from a life-threatening dependency on it, he said the feeling was partly one of "revenge." When asked why he wanted revenge on strangers, he wasn't able to say at first, but then he finally said,

> *They reminded me of my mother, my father, my uncle. Idiots who would do anything to get high. They were ruining their lives like my family did. I guess I was angry at my family for letting me down. Selling drugs to other addicts was kind of like spitting in their faces, saying, "Why don't you have more of the stuff that's destroying you? Maybe it's all you deserve!"*

DEALER, ADDICT

Jimmy may not have escaped dealing and gangs so easily if he had been using crack. Then he would have had to continue to associate with the crack world in order to get the substance. Something similar happened to a young man who calls himself T.Love and lives in New York City. T. Love is 25 years old. During the mid-eighties, at the age of 15, he fled to Manhattan from his mother's apartment in Jersey City, New Jersey, because she was abusing him whenever she got drunk.

Unlike Jimmy, T. Love found himself drawn toward drug abuse as a way of avoiding the pain he felt. He'd been smoking angel dust, or PCP, since the age of eleven. He liked the numbed, other-worldly feeling it produced. It made him feel invulnerable. When T. Love arrived in Manhattan, he went straight to the Port Authority Bus Terminal. He'd been there many times. It was an unofficial hangout for the homeless, a lot of whom were teenagers and a lot of whom were interested in drugs.

After camping out in the bus terminal for a day and a half, T. Love ran into a friend from Jersey City who took him to his "crib" in Spanish Harlem for some "dust." The crib was actually an apartment rented by a hairdresser called Tomorrow. Tomorrow supplemented his earnings by selling angel dust. He also rented out the boys as male prostitutes. A lot of the boys had connections to a gang from the Bronx known as the Savage Nomads. The heyday of the Savage Nomads had been in the seventies, but some still went around wearing their colors. In certain neighborhoods, especially in the Bronx, they ran small drug-dealing operations, one of which was the sale of angel dust.

The Savage Nomads thought T. Love could be a low-salaried dealer of angel dust because he'd be satisfied to be paid partially in drugs. They set him up on a corner in the Bronx to deal angel dust. At night he crashed at Tomorrow's and made extra money as a prostitute.

Today, at 25, T. Love is an upholsterer with a stable home, a wife, and a daughter. But it took three and a half years at a residential drug treatment program called Phoenix House for him to start moving toward this point. At the time, he couldn't have put what he was doing into words. But now he enjoys the sense of clarity it gives him to describe what he was doing and to make others understand.

The people T. Love thought cared most about him didn't really care. He'd tried to think of the Savage Nomads as the family he'd never had. Now he has seen through the fantasy of family they created and come to the conclusion that they were just using him to make a profit.

With the G's there was all this talk about "the family." "We look out for you." I swallowed all of it because I wanted a father, a big brother, so

G's who participate in illegal activities find that many parts of the business are out of their control. Often low-level gang members are jailed while high-ranking leaders go free.

bad. It doesn't matter if what he's telling you to do doesn't make sense. It's just good to have somebody there. At Phoenix House I had to admit that these people really weren't looking out for me. They were using me. They wanted somebody to push the dust on the street and bring in the bucks. I can't really blame them that much, they were addicts just like me. They needed to believe in family, too. They just didn't know what one was. They just knew how to "go for theirs."

T. Love stayed in the dealing and prostitution business until he was 19. Then Tomorrow got busted for promoting the prostitution of a minor. Suddenly T. Love found himself without a place to sleep. The "family" of G's affiliated with the Savage Nomads told him that they couldn't have "a dusthead crashing with us 24 X 7." So T. Love ended up sleeping at the top of the stairwell of Tomorrow's building in the dead of winter. It was after that experience that he decided to enter Phoenix House.

T. Love points out that there were many times during his four-year period as a dealer-prostitute that the whole thing seemed hollow and depressing.

But his addiction kept him glued to the source of his drug. Regardless of how disappointing his lifestyle became, he was afraid to face his own feelings without being high. Thus, long after he realized that his gang buddies weren't real family, he stuck with them out of the ingrained habit of drug abuse. He had to hit bottom before he could break away.

UNPREDICTABLE CONSEQUENCES OF GANG INVOLVEMENT

The truth of the matter is that very few "G's" ever get an intimate knowledge of their gang's connection to big business. If you join a gang with ties to a larger nation, you may be supporting activities of a business or political nature that you are not at all aware of. Most G's waste away as pawns doing their small part to keep these empires functioning. Those who do rise in the ranks are usually trapped forever because they know too much. They go on to a life of full-time crime and spend long periods in prison.

In May of 1991, a twenty-five-year-old battle between federal prosecutors and the El Rukns gang came to a head. Twenty-one defendants, many of them high-ranking leaders of the gang, were charged with trafficking narcotics, terrorism, racketeering, and murder. What came out in the trial was that this gang was like a loose corporation. Its tentacles extended throughout the country and had affected the lives of thousands of people. At one time the gang had about 5,000 members. The variety of its activities is mind-boggling. For example, their leader received an eighty-year prison sentence for seeking $2.5 million from the government of Libya in exchange for the gang's carrying out terrorist acts in the U.S.

How the gang spread and prospered was especially shocking. They purchased an old theater in Chicago and said it was their temple. Under this religious guise they commanded a growing drug operation on Chicago's West Side. Such a mode of operation is typical of other large nation-gangs. Sometimes they start as legitimate organizations before they become corrupt. For example, the Latin Kings began as a Latino fraternal organization in the 1940s. The name resurfaced in the prison system of Connecticut in the early 1990s. Both the Latin Kings and a black prison gang called The Nation distributed letters in prison to recruit members. From the way the letters read, both organizations seemed like well-meaning fraternities that stressed ethnic pride and the skills of self-reliance. But the Narcotics and Vice Division of the Bridgeport, Connecticut, police department has proof otherwise. They have seized thousands of guns and narcotics from these so-called benevolent organizations. What is more, no gang Nation is really very centralized. What's promised by one faction may be contradicted by another.

SAYING NO TO GANG BUSINESS

Even a small clique or crew can have informal connections to larger operations—drug dealing, smuggling, or even terrorism. Especially if your gang is making money illegally, it probably answers to dangerous "higher-ups." Before you go looking for family or easy money in the business-oriented gang, keep the following points in mind:

Gangs don't really share the wealth. Most G's are masters of the soft sell. Don't be fooled by statements claiming that "we're all in this together." In most gangs, a few leaders make huge profits by exploiting a large work force. Even if your friends who are involved in gang business seem to have a lot of ready cash and nice clothes, ask yourself what will happen to them when they want to stop dealing. Remember the stories in this chapter in which dealers were used and mistreated by gangs through well-timed lies and manipulation. Also keep in mind that your fantasies of a one-person operation could come to an abrupt end if a gang decides you are infringing on its turf. Avoid all offers of easy money. They rarely turn out to be true.

THE FACTS ABOUT ILLEGAL BUSINESS

If you are thinking about making money through illegal operations, statistics say that:

• Your income will never be steady. Even though you may have periods of high income, you will also go through periods with next to nothing.
• You will spend time in prison. If you have children or any dependent relatives, they are likely to suffer during this period in which you cannot support them.
• Your chances of getting killed are several times that of the person not involved in illegal activities, even if both of you live in the same high-risk neighborhood.
• If you want to move into legitimate work later in life, you may not be able to. You won't have the work skills or social skills.

Ambition can be a positive, motivating force. But never close your eyes to where it is leading you. Face the facts when you decide you want to make money. Do it the right way.

What you sell matters. If you sell drugs, firearms, or other illegal things you are definitely hurting a lot of people. Crack is highly addictive and eventually decreases a person's ability to feel pleasure. Heroin is addictive and can kill. Both drugs destroy brain tissue and other organ tissues in the body. Marijuana impairs memory and interferes with learning. Angel dust can cause convulsions, brain damage, or death. What you sell may one day get into the hands of people you care about. It may destroy an entire community. You will have to take part of the responsibility for the problems it causes.

When you deal drugs, you are taking an active role in destroying the lives and neighbor-hoods of your own community.

A drug problem can enslave you. Dealing drugs is dangerous. If you deal drugs because you want drugs, you are probably an addict. Otherwise, why would you put your life in danger just to get high? If you are an addict, you'll be enmeshed in the drug business long after it stops being fun. You won't be able to quit because you will need to keep connected to the supply. If you are an addict, you won't be able to cure yourself on your own. You'll have to investigate drug treatment programs and recovery groups to get off drugs. If you are an addict who is involved in dealing drugs, a residential drug treatment program might be just what you need. It will get you away from the people you work for so that they can't take revenge on you for quitting. In the meantime, you can go through recovery and evaluate your situation more clearly.

Gang business affairs are out of your control. The quick money you get from dealing drugs, shaking down businesses, robbery, or other illegal activities may provide you with temporary surges of feeling powerful. But when you do business with gangs, you are more likely to be in a powerless situation. They can change the terms of your employment at any time. Frightening, uncontrollable forces having to do with smuggling, extortion, terrorism, or drug wars may sweep you up as well. Gang business is an unpredictable investment.

There are other ways to make money. There are laws in this country to protect workers who have legal jobs. Gang business is quick money, high risk, and statistically doomed to failure. Legitimate jobs are a slower way of making money, low risk, and potentially more and more profitable. Minimum wage may be frustrating, but it won't get you killed. Legitimate jobs often offer other benefits such as on-the-job training, health insurance, paid vacations, and guaranteed promotions for meeting certain standards. When you get a legitimate job, you agree to a salary and other conditions. These can't be changed without notice. If you want to quit, there will be no vendettas against you. Check out the job market. You may find that doing business with gangs is not your only alternative.

6

GETTING OUT AND STAYING OUT

I want to jump out of the gang.
—Alfonso, age 16

What about those few G's who rose to the top of gangland and were able to put their hands on huge sums of money? Did they ever regret their gang involvement? How does long-term, even successful, gang life affect a person after many years? Is it possible to leave a gang?

T. Rodgers is almost as well known as some movie stars in Los Angeles. Legend has it that he is the founder of the megagang, the Bloods, which turned parts of L.A. into a battlefield when the Bloods opposed the other megagang, the Crips. At one point, he was at the top of the Los Angeles crack trade. He also earned thousands and thousands of dollars as a pimp. Anyone with gang-banging ambitions would hold Rodgers to be a hero, a model of how far a G can go.

Rodgers started his meteoric career as a big-time G early. At 16, he commanded about 500 homeboy G's who belonged to his gang. The first time he got shot was that same year, which was in the early seventies. Rodgers was alone when four gang-bangers took a potshot at him from a car. The shot gouged his scalp and produced a lot of blood, but it wasn't really life-threatening. He knew it was dangerous for him to go out alone. His gang had already made a lot of enemies. The second time he got shot was just six months later. This time the wound was

The violence of gangs has gotten so out of control that some gang leaders are seeking ways to stop it peacefully.

more serious. The bullet burrowed a large hole in one buttock. Two years later, at the age of 18, he had been shot a total of four times.

Ironically, Rodgers's gang career started out when his mother brought him to L.A. in 1969 to escape the gang violence of Chicago. Little did she know that he was carrying a charter to establish a West Coast version of the Blackstone Rangers, a Chicago gang. The Crips were already established when Rodgers came to town. They told him that he and his gang had to give up their gear and change their name to Crips. Rodgers and his G's refused. Soon their gang became known as the Almighty Black P. Stones. The Almighty Black P. Stones took over their school, Dorsey High, and turned it into "Do-or-die Dorsey."

Meanwhile the Crips were recruiting new members all through the seventies. (The Crips began around 1968. Ironically, the gang grew out of the fights that broke out at dances organized to help keep young people off the streets and out of trouble.) By the summer of 1974, the Crips had a powerful army. As their activities expanded, shootings became common in Rodgers's neighborhood. In his own grab for more power, Rodgers started inviting kids who were fed up with getting beat down by the Crips to join his gang. He showed them where to find guns and where to get rid of them in a hurry when it was necessary.

Rodgers was a born "executive" of the type of big-business gang you read about in the last chapter. Since ninth grade, he'd been making money from drug-dealing, stolen cars, extortion, and even murder-for-hire. He had a huge work force carrying out these operations. He was still in junior high school but he was making tens of thousands of dollars. He showed it off, too, buying tailored suits and even top hats, having himself photographed with over $30,000 in hundred dollar bills piled on a bed in front of him.

THE BIRTH OF THE BLOODS

About 1974, the association of gangs that Rodgers had got going started calling itself "the Bloods." Rodgers made sure that he wrote the charter. He wanted to be the one who made the rules. One requirement was that every G sign the charter in his own blood.

You'd think that rising to the top of the gang world would have satisfied Rodgers. After all, from the time he was 9 years old it had been his sole ambition. It may even be yours. But strangely enough, the very growth of his group is what alienated Rodgers from gang life. The Blackstone Rangers had been a neighborhood-style gang. It was about fraternity, survival, and business. Now, even though Rodgers was Number One with the Bloods, he realized he had lost control of his purposes. He knew that "a boss of all bosses wouldn't last two minutes . . ." in L.A. His power was awesome but shaky. What is more, although the Blackstone Rangers had sold drugs, they had strictly forbidden their G's to use them. As membership in the Bloods mushroomed, all of that changed. Rodgers lost control. G's started thinking how they lived was their own business. Rodgers saw boys that he had conscripted peering behind a loaded gun with stoned eyes and hands trembling from cocaine. He realized he'd made a big mistake.

What happened to Rodgers is representative of what finally happens to a lot of gangland's top gangsters. The means they use to obtain the money and power they dreamed about start backfiring on them. The poison in their own merchandise—drugs—starts destroying the ranks from within. The empire gets out of control.

For Rodgers, one of the most demoralizing aspects of the empire he had to take responsibility for building was the new emphasis on drive-by shootings. "That was my strictest [rule]," he told a reporter. "No goddam drive-bys. Ever. Period. A drive-by's the worst thing ever invented—it drove me out of 'banging faster than all that other crap put together."

Rodgers's disgust with what happened to the world he had helped build made him leave gang-banging at the ripe old age of 18. Unfortunately, his skills and his attitude were still the same. He'd been making money from illegal activities since the age of 9. He was used to the quick profits and fly-by-night operations. That is probably why he discovered a new talent in pimping. With a stable of young women working under him as prostitutes, he raised his standard of living even higher. He became known throughout Los Angeles as a man who gave lavish parties, owned several mansions, and bought a new car every month.

In the 1980s, cocaine, and then crack, became closely associated with the world of prostitution. By this time, Rodgers's big-time business skills were at their peak. Pushing the thought that crack might be the deadliest drug yet to hit the streets out of his mind, he worked quickly to control a large portion of the trade. He had to shut his eyes to the devastation caused by the drug that he saw all around him. But he'd had plenty of practice at turning off his feelings when large profits were at stake.

"Crack put the gang thing over the top," says Rodgers. "I mean, it was plenty wild before crack, but I could at least talk to these bad boys." He was right. Crack put things so over the top that young children started getting strung out on it. By that time, Rodgers had several children of his own. Taking care of them gave him a sense of family that was precious to him. The fact that his cocaine operations were eating away at the lives of other children and families in the community started to keep him up at night. After twenty years of crime, Rodgers had come face-to-face with himself. He didn't like the picture.

A HOLLOW SUCCESS

Rodgers admits that it was at those high points in his career as a gangster that he felt the most hollow, that life seemed the most meaningless. In a brutal way, he found out that the hungry heart that comes with poverty cannot be cured with money alone. The phases in his career are interesting. At the very moment that he accomplished his first goal, to unite L.A.'s G's into a megagang, he had second thoughts. Instead of it being the realization of his wildest dreams, it was the beginning of a demoralizing downer. But it was too late to reverse what he had done. The effects of it are still being felt today on the streets of L.A. and other American cities.

To avoid facing what he'd done to the streets of L.A., Rodgers immersed himself in another criminal world where the damage was not yet so obvious. As a pimp he could blend business with pleasure and luxuries to create a false image of paradise. His lavish parties made him feel generous. But was he? The proof that he was just "out for his" came soon when cocaine hit the trade. Rodgers just couldn't get out of the cycle of using others for his personal gain, even when he'd gone way beyond the level of mere survival. Finally, Rodgers began to see himself as a "child killer" because younger and younger people were becoming enslaved by crack. He had always known that gangs were made up of a lot of kids who had no father to turn to and that the gangs served as substitute families for those who came from families that were torn apart. At the height of his power in the cocaine business, he again came to an impasse. He just couldn't go on.

THE BLOODS AND THE CRIPS LEGACY

To date, the war between the Bloods and the Crips in Los Angeles has claimed about 3,000 lives and wounded or crippled thousands of others. Wheelchairs are a common sight in South Central Los Angeles, where most of the gang-banging takes place. Blood vs. Crip competition has spread up and down the West Coast, from San Diego to Seattle. In L.A. alone, there may be as many as 100,000 gang-bangers affiliated with these two groups.

Here are some current facts about the Bloods and the Crips:
• Chapters also exist in Phoenix, Albuquerque, Denver, Omaha, Houston, Amarillo, and Colorado Springs.
• Chapters in the heavily Mormon city of Salt Lake City are thought to be partly responsible for a tripling of the crime rate there between 1992 and 1993.
• In York, Pennsylvania, the Crips were selling $40,000 worth of crack per week by 1988.
• In Los Angeles County, there are about 157,000 Crips and Bloods members in 1,100 chapters and related gangs who kill each other at a rate of two per day and get arrested at the rate of 50,000 per year.

When Rodgers realized he could no longer face dealing drugs, his life underwent a radical transformation. He decided to face his feelings. Memories of a father who both abused and abandoned him welled up in his mind. He admitted the pain of feeling frightened and defenseless in front of the very man who was supposed to protect him. With these feelings in mind, Rodgers stopped dealing drugs and started seeking out young people who were going through what he had endured. He found them in the very junior high and high schools he had attended. Back then, he had turned their playgrounds into jungles. Now he was appearing in their auditoriums to packed assemblies, telling the real truth about gang-banging.

In his speeches to students about the price of gang involvement, Rodgers let his emotions run free. When he described the death of homies, tears flowed from his eyes. He even showed the wounds he had on various parts of his body. The effect was phenomenal. That the "baddest G" in all of L.A. had the courage to bare his soul before hundreds seemed astounding. His audiences were spellbound.

However, Rodgers felt that talking at school assemblies wasn't enough. That is about the time when he met ex-football star Jim Brown, who was trying to start an organization to rehabilitate young people who had been involved in gangs. The two met in 1988. Within four years Brown's organization had a name—the Amer-I-Can Program—and was established in five states. Rodgers's role, as Jim Brown put it, was to "go into the worst places in America and convert the baddest gangsters there to what we were doing." Brown felt that Rodgers was perfect for the task since he was seen as a leader by gang members throughout the country.

Once Rodgers had recruited kids from the streets, the Amer-I-Can program really went into effect. Stage one was some hard, plain talk about individual responsibility. Brown felt that the gang members had to take all the responsibility for the way they were living instead of focusing the blame on bad parents, societal prejudice, or other factors. Once they were willing to do that, Brown enrolled them in an intensive ninety-hour course for success. Using many teachers who themselves were ex-gang members and ex-cons, the course taught fundamental life-management skills, such as how to speak clearly, how to handle your feelings without resorting to violence, how to present yourself for a job interview, and how to open a checking account. These are basic survival skills for the real world, but because most of the G's had spent most of their time in gangs or in jail, they had never learned them.

Rodgers is still a big man in his neighborhood. But he uses his clout to talk to kids who are making the wrong decisions. His new role has made him even more respected on the streets of L.A. Even G's who don't want to change show respect as his car pulls to the curb. For the first time in Rodgers's life, he is not living a contradiction.

A CHANGE OF HEART

The next time Rodgers visits Jim Brown at home, he has a chance of running into someone who used to be his mortal enemy. The man's name is Gregory Davis, and he was one of the major players in the early days of the legendary Crips. In 1995, at the age of 40, Davis is the "graduate" of 15 years in prison for assault, robbery, and murder. Anyone who looks at Davis immediately picks up clues about the past he has led. Falling from his left eye are three tattooed tear drops in memory of three friends whom he lost to gunfire.

These days, Davis spends a lot of time picking up free paint from hardware stores to cover up the fresh gang graffiti sprayed all over the buildings of his block. Still living in South Central Los Angeles, Davis says he is sick and tired of "all these gunshots, all these helicopters flying." So tired is he that he devotes part of every week to his job as an anti-gang counselor.

Davis lacks job skills because he devoted his entire youth and young manhood to gang activity. But in an attempt to become self-sufficient he has developed a business selling large decorative mirrors that are personalized by hand for the client. Davis is also involved with Brown's Amer-I-Can. That both he and Rodgers can work for peace with the same organization is a strong message to those Bloods and Crips who still think of each other as enemies. It shows that any conflict can eventually be resolved and that even your worst enemy may end up as a friend.

ENDING THE MADNESS

What would happen if other gang leaders had a change of heart? If they were to take a stand, would the ranks follow? On Mexican Independence Day in 1994, representatives from every Latino gang on Los Angeles's West Side came together in the town of Venice. They came not to fight, but to give awards to the notable peace-keepers of their neighborhoods. The occasion was the third year of peace after the signing of the Sureno truce. The truce had effectively put an end to violence among Latinos.

Gang truces save lives, but the gangs themselves would not have to exist if young people had other alternatives. That's what Gang Peace is all about. The organization was started in Boston by a recovering drug addict named Rodney Dailey. Dailey knew all too well what a path with few choices could do to a life. He had experienced it firsthand when he turned to drugs to avoid psychological pain and then slowly but surely saw his options becoming limited.

Dailey goes right into the streets of troubled neighborhoods in Boston and talks to young people on a one-to-one basis. "I say to them, 'You're worth more than this,'" explained Daily. "The message is that life is more than a drug

After decades of feuding, the Crips and the Bloods in the Watts section of Los Angeles have made a truce to stop the bloodshed.

game, and that life is more valuable than cash. I try to tell them that if we keep killing ourselves off, it's a form of genocide."

Dailey used his own money to found Gang Peace, but now it runs on annual donations and grants of about $180,000. Its focus is on business, and it stresses that the best way to do business is with an education. Gang Peace offers anyone who asks thirty-two free hours of college courses through a computer hookup with Atlantic Union College in Boston. It also helps its members find summer jobs. A few years ago, it even placed a few ex-G's in paying video-production internships at the Boston Film-Video Foundation. With the aid of the community, Gang Peace has set up support groups, a summer concert program, and a small recording studio for neighborhood rap groups.

The secret of Gang Peace's success with some young people may be that it does not preach. Instead of approaching a gang member with a critical, negative attitude about gangs, people working for Gang Peace come with helpful advice, such as information about AIDS or first-aid measures for stopping the bleeding caused by gunshot wounds. Gang members aren't pressured to leave their gangs. However, many of them eventually come to realize that the same skills they've been using in negative ways to deal drugs or wage turf wars can be shaped into good business skills. And the program seems to be working. Between 1990 and 1991 while Gang Peace did its work, homicides dropped 25 percent citywide and 53 percent in gang-ridden neighborhoods.

Gangs can direct their activities in positive directions. Here young members of the Vice Lords talk to schoolchildren about self-respect and pride.

Perhaps one of the most controversial projects designed to end gang violence was instituted in Fort Worth, Texas. In 1994, the city council passed a measure that actually hired six gang leaders to convince fellow gang members to stop performing criminal acts. The gang leaders were all trained in dispute mediation and were sent back to the streets with their message of peace. Programs such as this are very controversial because they sometimes backfire. Some gang leaders have said they were working for peace but instead used their jobs to get information about competing gangs in order to strengthen their own crews.

THE POLICE TAKE ACTION

Perhaps no one but gang members themselves has a closer look at what's going on in the gang world than law enforcers and people working in the penal system. Over the years, these people have come to realize that routine investigation, arrest, prosecution, and punishment are not working to lower the incidence of gang-related crime. Since then, a variety of methods for controlling gangs have been tried by law enforcement agencies throughout the United States.

In several cities around the nation, the police, prison officials, and school administrators have experimented with stricter monitoring of schools, housing projects, and prisons to prevent gangs from forming. For example, in Connecticut, all in-mates' phone calls are now monitored to prevent gang-related information being passed from people convicted of gang-related crimes to contacts on the outside. This plan is considered controversial, and the Connecticut Civil Liberties Union is fighting it in court, saying that it is unconstitutional and violates state wiretapping laws. However, correctional officials claim the program helped them prevent a major gang confrontation at one of the state's largest prisons in 1994.

Many schools now keep up to date on gang insignia and gang colors, which they forbid within the school grounds. Gang-related graffiti is removed from the school grounds

AN IN-YOUR-FACE APPROACH

Sick of seeing kids killed by gang violence, an Indiana funeral director named Michael Bluitt announced plans to bring a warning into the schools. He rigged up a coffin with a mirror so that kids would see their own faces when they peeked inside. The purpose is to turn kids on to the reality of death so that they will think twice before becoming involved in gang violence.

Said Bluitt, "Youth have this idea from their videos and music that death is glamorous and it is an honor. But death isn't like television where you just get a little blood on your shirt."

as soon as possible, and anyone seen applying it is disciplined. Some schools have also stepped up security by installing improved metal detectors to prevent students from coming to school with weapons and by searching lockers on a regular basis for drugs, weapons, or other gang-related items. In Wilmington, California, Gulf Avenue School sponsors the Harbor Area Gang Alternatives Program. The program keeps archives on graffiti writers, seeks them out, and confronts them. It also offers classroom instruction on how to avoid gangs.

In a housing project in Chicago, authorities started a controversial instant-search procedure, allowing them to enter and search any apartment without notice if criminal activity is suspected. Like the monitoring of telephone calls in the Connecticut prisons, this practice is being opposed by some residents of the housing project who feel it violates their civil rights.

In a few large cities, police are using sophisticated computer programming to monitor gang leaders and gang members. Information on gangs and profiles of those involved are fed into the computers daily. Eventually, a total picture of criminal connections is obtained. Police can use it to make multiple arrests connected to a single incident.

Because of gang violence, students at many schools must now be searched with metal detectors before entering the building.

Meanwhile, in January 1992, the Federal Bureau of Investigation assigned 300 of its agents to the investigation of urban street gangs. This agency has extensive experience keeping tabs on organized crime and hopes to apply some of the techniques it has learned to large networks of gangs. In the weeks after the Los Angeles riots, the FBI joined forces with other law enforcers to identify and prosecute those who had committed criminal acts. From a TV video they were able to identify some of the men who had violently beaten a truck driver as members of a particular gang.

The police are learning that early, intimate involvement with gang members and potential gang members pays off. Many large cities now have special gang units with officers who go into the community and deal with gang members on a one-to-one basis. They help cement truces between gangs, prevent vendettas, and gather information on criminal activity. This works to the extent that gang members and other young people trust them. Understanding this, they have combined police work with fathering, community activism, and helping the families of those exposed to gangs.

In the early 1990s in Los Angeles, the police department began a privately funded experiment called the Jeopardy program. This program was designed to work with at-risk young people to keep them from falling into the hands of gangs in the first place. The program uses a variety of approaches. The police personally go to the homes of individual children who are chronically truant and take them to school. They counsel teachers and parents about coping with gangs and the gang mentality. They provide athletic programs for those children who become interested.

GETTING OUT

Gang truces save lives, but they won't get you out of a gang. It is possible, though, to turn your life around if you really want to. Alfonso F. joined a small all-black gang in Syracuse, New York, at the age of 13. He remembers exactly what attracted him to it:

> We was living in the fifteenth ward which is mostly all black people. Syracuse is up north but they still got a big ghetto there. The winters are harsh and cold. Well, every time I would walk to school, there was a gang called the Wallabees that starts pelting me with iceballs—that's snowballs melted down and packed really hard so that they almost solid ice. Well one time, they hit me upside the head with one of them iceballs and I was down in the snow, out cold for a couple a minutes. They just leaves me there. If I hadn't come to then maybe I would have frozen to death. Well when I did come to, I drag myself back to the house and my cousin, from Buffalo, who was 16, a dropout, is visiting. I told him what they did to me and he takes a big silver gun out of his suitcase, puts it in my hand and says, "Do that feel good to you? 'Cause that's power. And if you was holding this, wouldn't be no ice-ball hitting you upside the head." Well, he told me he was a member of the Shirttails and that he come to Syracuse to start a chapter here. So he got me and I got a few other kids together, guys and girls, and we formed the Shirttails of Syracuse. We only had but one gun but we passed it. Everybody got to hold it a day or two a month. Well, word gets around about who we are now and what we packing. Nobody ever hit me with any iceball then.

The Shirttails lasted for approximately three years. They never acquired more guns, but they did develop an income selling small amounts of crack in their neighborhood and in one other neighborhood in Syracuse. Then Alfonso was offered a chance for a community scholarship to a technical school in Syracuse. He knew that in order to do it he'd have to change his lifestyle. Gang life was based on constantly changing hours. Sometimes he'd be up all night dealing and sometimes he'd sleep all day. It was also unpredictable. A number of times he'd had to drop everything and run to a location where a member of his gang was in trouble.

I calls up my cousin in Buffalo and I says to him, "I want out. I want out of the Shirttails." Well, you shoulda heard him. He was saying the only way you going to get out is as a dead man. You a Shirttail for life. Well, we musta talked for maybe five minutes before he hung up on me. So I took the bus to Buffalo and walked right in on him. I made him look at me and I said, "I thought you was family and I thought you said family was taking care of yours. I got a chance to do something; what kind of protection you offering me saying I can't do it?" After a while, he come round. He says, "You family and I'm gonna say O.K., but somebody else I wouldn't let him." Then I did something I wasn't sure if it was right. I went to a cop that had brought me in a whole bunch of times. I knew him. I said, "Listen, I ain't coming to you as no snitch. I ain't going to tell you nothing about the Shirttails. I'm coming to you so you can help me make one less Shirttail. I just want you to keep an eye on me for about a week. I want to jump out of the gang." You know what he did? He stood in front of my house for four days even off of work, and when a Shirttail come around and says, "Where Alfonso, I got to speak to him," he says, "He's under guard. Do you want to be arrested?" Well, you

Police methods against gangs have become more sophisticated and effective.

wouldn't believe how fast they forgot about me. If we was still in the same school it would have been different. But now that they was still in high school and I was going to technical school they put me in a different world. I haven't hung out with them since.

HOW YOU CAN GET OUT

Alfonso was both lucky and good at strategy. The fact that he was changing schools made it easier for him to disassociate from his gang. He also had the good luck of knowing a rather exceptional cop. Alfonso was careful to cover the same base twice, first by talking to his cousin, and then by getting the help of the police. He actually trusted neither implicitly and used them as a check on one another as well as double insurance of protection.

What should you do if you are involved with a gang and want to get out? The solutions vary according to the situation, but no situation is hopeless. As you make your moves, keep the following pointers in mind. Some of them may be totally inappropriate for your purposes, but some may work:

Talk honestly to other G's about your feelings and values. In some cases, there really may be a way to explain to other gang members that your feelings and values have changed and that it is time for you to move on. You will have to do this without seeming critical of them. People often join gangs because they seek friendship and an escape from their feelings of low self-esteem. They can be extremely touchy and combative when it comes to discussing ideas or values. Nevertheless, if you earnestly explain what alternatives you think life holds, they may come to some understanding of your new goals. If they don't, drop it. Don't escalate the discussion to any level that threatens your safety.

Appeal to a relative, guardian, or friend. Relatives, guardians, and friends can help in a number of ways. Just think about it. If you have a relative in the same gang as yourself, that relative might be able to offer you protection as you distance yourself from the gang. He or she may be able to instruct the other members not to take reprisal or try to prevent you from leaving. Try, as well, to think of some adult whom you trust who has connections to the legal system, the social services system, or your school system. That person can go to the right people on your behalf and demand protection from gang violence. He or she may be able to help you transfer schools or leave the neighborhood if things really come to that. You know the atmosphere of your gang and the people around you better than anyone. So act cautiously.

Talk to the police. This isn't about being a snitch. There are police officers, detectives, and counselors in the gang units of most urban police systems set up to handle gang problems. If there is one you feel confident about, you might want to feel him or her out. You don't have to give much information or tell your intent immediately, but if you discover someone who you think understands your situation, that person may be able to help. The police can counsel you about the safest way of distancing yourself from a gang. They can get in touch with teachers, your parents, the parents of other gang members, or the gang members themselves. They may even be able to mediate a discussion between you and other gang members and help draw up a signed agreement formally letting you out of the gang. Again, take stock of the entire situation before you take action.

Become an activist. Admittedly, this takes a special kind of personality. However, suppose you were to bring change and new ideas to your gang rather than slipping out of it and leaving it in the lurch. You may have some positive ideas that can shape your gang into a healthy, productive, and supportive social group. Brainstorm some legal ways for all of you to make money. Get some books, comics, or reading material on the true meaning of friendship. Find a project that you can all do together, such as repairing an old community center or painting a clubhouse. Research your ethnic history and share the information.

You know the people in your gang. You might want to introduce these ideas slowly to them, a little at a time. Or you might want to attempt a "revolution" of ideas, catching them by surprise with positive ideas and a new way of doing things.

AVOIDING GANGS

To avoid gangs, you must look outside and inside. You've got to see through the lies about friendship, power, riches, and excitement that gangs use to attract new members. You also have to see who you are and what your needs are. This can be painful. Some of your needs may temporarily make you feel vulnerable and frightened. But once you've admitted them, you can go about satisfying them in a realistic way. Here are some key questions to ask yourself the moment you feel attracted to a gang:

What happened to the other members? Do a little investigating. Are any members in jail? Dead? Crippled? What do their families think of their gang involvement? Are they happy about it? How is their schoolwork doing? What are their plans for the future? In most cases, you'll find that the answers are rather depressing. The allure of the gang won't be the same as it was.

What can I really do about racism? Are you thinking of joining a gang because your ethnic group is being dumped on by people in the neighborhood or by society? Turf wars will only solve the problem temporarily. Then it will get worse. Talk to your teacher and your librarian about racism. Find out what a "hate crime" is. There are new laws protecting people against crimes committed out of racial hatred. You may be able to use them to protect yourself. At any rate, keep in mind that feelings of racial pride and feelings of racial superiority are

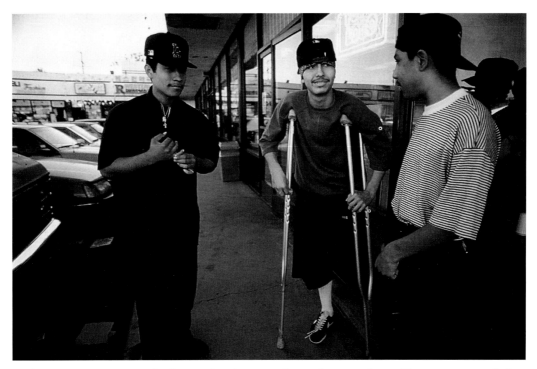

Before you join a gang, find out what happened to other members. Chances are good that some are dead, crippled, or in jail.

two different things. If you join a gang based on the idea of the superiority of your ethnic group, you will become just as bigoted as those who oppressed you in the first place.

What's home like? If your home life is violent or insecure or if your parent or parents are intoxicated or absent a great deal of the time, you need to do something about it. You can appeal for help from the social service system, your school, or the police department. You can form friendships with sympathetic teachers, counselors, coaches, or members of the clergy. Look for the right person. He or she will make a better "big brother" or "big sister" than gang leaders. He or she won't demand absolute obedience and won't let you down when you are in trouble.

Am I giving in to peer pressure? Every time you do something because the other kids are doing it, you succumb to peer pressure. If every "cool" kid in your school is walking around with a specific tattoo and the same two colors, it is natural that you might feel an urge for the same symbols. It will take a lot of strength of character to go your own way and resist the temptation to join their gang. It might help to think about developing other social groups outside of those in school. Look around the neighborhood, your extended family, your community centers, or your place of worship. Actively seek out your own friends and your own group. Stand tall and strong and think for yourself.

What's the best way for me to get money? You may need money now, and you may have fantasies about what it would be like to have a lot of it later. These are good motivators for hard work and hard study. The next time you admire an expensive coat on someone else, think about what kinds of jobs pay the money to buy something like that. Could you ever be working at one of those jobs? Investigate the qualifications for those jobs and work toward your goal. The next time you are tempted by easy money, think about jail "fashions." Jail uniforms are pretty basic. You're not even allowed to wear a belt. They're all the same and they are not of the best quality.

What's the best way to get real love and respect? This might be the most difficult question you ever ask yourself. The fact that young people in search of warmth, love, and a sense of belonging end up bleeding to death on the sidewalk is an irony almost too terrible to bear. However, once you admit that, like everybody else, you want love and respect, you can choose the most effective way of getting them.

Love and respect from others may not be available at home or in school. Your neighborhood may not be a place where they are often expressed. But they do exist in the world, and you are definitely worthy of them. You will get love from people who respect themselves and respect others, not those who are obsessed with showing the world that they have power.

THE FREEDOM TO CHOOSE

There is a kind of love in the solidarity of gang members, but it is too often snuffed out by the violent situations they get themselves into. There is a kind of courage in the gang-banger. However, because it's based on rage and feelings of low self-esteem, it becomes a destructive courage. There is pride in the gang that fights to keep its turf, but that pride is so fragile it can be extinguished the moment the other gang is on top. There are riches to be had in gang life, but they come from exploiting others and they can be lost in the blink of an eye.

If you choose not to look for solidarity, courage, pride, and riches in the world of gangs, you may find that others will choose with you. It won't be easy to go against the flow, but in the end it will pay off. Can you resist the temptation of the youth gang? It all depends on how much courage you really have, how proud you really are, and how rich you are in spirit.

Felipe Velez, the ex-leader of San Francisco's Diamond Heights Gang now writes poetry about his experiences.

The Cross on the Hand
by Felipe Ulloa Velez

While you lay
in that coffin
with a cross on your hand
I can only pray
in vain
that it won't happen again.

Not even out of high school
and already visiting the pearly
gates.

A priest whispers Hail Marys
while all the tuffs
teary eyed
plan a pay back.

The baby face
in the coffin
stiff and pale
dreams drained.

A young father pleads and yells
"Stop it!"

Youth unmoved.

Death, death
is all they see.

The fun of friends
turned lethal.

The importance of life
not fully understood.

Simple plans
become mind bending
decisions.

Eye for an eye
a painless decree.

In broad daylight
the next day
bang, bang
another dead.

A pact till the end
with a cross
on his hand.

ADDITIONAL RESOURCES

800 numbers are toll-free calls. There is no charge for calling a telephone number that begins with 1-800.

Alanon and Alateen
1-800-356-9996
(Support groups for the family members of alcoholics)

Alcohol and Drug Help
1-800-821-HELP

Foresters National Child Abuse Hotline
1-800-4-A-CHILD
1-800-2-A-CHILD

Civil Rights Hotline
1-800-368-1019
(in Washington, D.C.: 1-202-863-1019)

Cocaine Hotline
1-800- COCAINE

Contact Literacy Hotline
1-800-228-8813
1-800-552-9097

Equal Employment Opportunity Commission
1-800-669-4000

"Just Say No" International
1-800-258-2766
(In California: 1-415-939-6666)

Hit Home
1-800-448-4663
(For runaways, gang problems)

National GED Info Hotline
1-800-626-9433
1-800-552-9097

National Domestic Violence Hotline
1-800-333-7233

National Hate Hotline
1-800-347-HATE

Problem Pregnancy Hotline
1-800-228-0332

Runaway's Hotline
1-800-231-6946
1-800-392-3352

WETIP Hotline
1-800-78-CRIME
(Offers rewards for tips on crimes being committed in your community.)

Organizations you can write to or call:

Center to Prevent Handgun Violence
1225 Eye St. NW, Suite 1100
Washington, D.C. 20005
(202) 289-7319

Delancey Street Foundation
2563 Divisadero Street
San Francisco, California 94115
(415) 957- 9800
(Aid to former convicts, substance abusers, and prostitutes.)

Male Youth Enhancement Project
1510 9th Street NW
Washington, DC 20001
(202) 332-0213

Martin Luther King Center for
Nonviolent Social Change
449 Auburn Ave. NE
Atlanta, Georgia 30312
(404) 524-1956

National Assault Prevention Center
P.O. Box 02005
Columbus, Ohio 43202
(614) 291-2540

National Coalition Against Domestic
Violence
P.O. Box 18749
Denver, Colorado 80218

National Crime Prevention Council
1700 K Street NW, Second Floor
Washington, DC 20006
(202) 466-6272

National Victim Center
307 West 7th Street, Suite 1001
Fort Worth, Texas 76102
(817) 877-3355

Resolving Conflict Creatively
163 Third Avenue, Suite 239
New York, New York 10009
(212) 260-6290

FOR FURTHER READING

Asbury, Herbert. Gangs of New York: *An Informal History of the New York Underworld.* New York: Dorset Press, 1990

Dawley, David. *A Nation of Lords: The Autobiography of the Vice Lords,* 2nd ed. Prospect Heights, IL: Waveland Press, 1992.

From Gangs to Grace: The Study Guide. Pomona, CA: Family and Community Educational Services, 1991.

Goldentyer, Debra. *Gangs.* Teen Hotline Series. Chatham, NJ: Raintree Steck-Vaughn, 1993.

Goldstein, Arnold P., and C. Ronald Huff, eds. *Gang Intervention Handbook.* Champaign, IL: Research Press, 1992.

Greenberg, Keith E. *Out of the Gang.* Minneapolis: Lerner Publications, 1992.

Kyte, Kathy S. *Play It Safe: The Kids' Guide to Personal Safety and Crime Prevention.* New York: Alfred A. Knopf, 1983.

Jackson, Robert K., and Wesley D. McBride, *Understanding Street Gangs.* Placerville, CA: Copperhouse, 1989.

Johnson, Darryl. *This Thing Called Gangs: A Guide in Recognizing the Danger Signs.* Topeka, KS: Lone Tree, 1992.

Knox, George. *An Introduction to Gangs.* Buchanan, MI: Vande Vere, 1991.

Korem, Dan. *Streetwise Parents, Foolproof Kids,* 2nd ed. Richardson, TX: International Focus Press, 1994.

Lawson, Ann. *Why Kids Join Gangs.* Edina, MN: Johnson Institute, 1994.

Redpath, Ann. *What Happens If You Join a Street Gang.* Mankato, MN: Capstone Press, 1995.

Miedzian, Myriam. *Boys Will Be Boys: Breaking the Link between Masculinity and Violence.* New York: Doubleday, 1991.

Rodriguez, Luis J. *Always Running: La Vida Loca: Gang Days in L.A.* New York: Simon & Schuster, 1994.

Stark, Evan. *Everything You Need to Know about Street Gangs.* New York: Rosen Group, 1992

GLOSSARY

Code. Set rules for behavior that express allegiance to certain beliefs or values. Most gangs have codes of dress, behavior, and even speech. Following codes expresses one's willingness to abide by the rules and values of a gang. The codes direct the behavior of gang members and make it easier for gang leaders to control them.

Colors. The particular combination of colors (usually two) worn by some gang members to symbolize their membership in a gang. Colors can appear in the clothing, accessories, cars, or even homes of gang members. Colors are closely tied to gang codes. They are the "flag" of gang membership and symbolize a set of values, beliefs, and rules to live by.

Crack. A highly concentrated, smokable form of cocaine. Pieces of crack usually look like small white pebbles. They are smoked in a glass stem, a pipe, or mixed with marijuana or tobacco. The rush sends an instant high to the user's brain, dangerously revving up all body systems. Crack is highly addictive.

Crew. A small, informal gang. A crew usually develops out of a small group of neighborhood friends united for a common purpose. If it grows and its rules become more formal, it is called a gang.

Ethnicity. The qualities that define a particular culture, including its language, dress, food, religious beliefs, and values. In the United States, which has many ethnicities, members of a particular ethnicity sometimes try to preserve that ethnicity's values and lifestyles. These values and lifestyles sometimes conflict with American daily life. Sometimes gangs form out of an attempt to deal with this conflict. Gangs sometimes are, in part, an attempt to assert ethnicity and stress the values of a particular minority culture.

Gang-banging. Fighting in a gang. Sometimes gang-banging has a particular purpose: to enact vengeance or to seize territory. At other times it is done as an expression of anger and aggression and for the temporary sense of power it brings.

Jump in or jump out. To induct or kick out a gang member. Jumping in usually takes the form of an initiation ceremony. The new gang member is brought into the gang and introduced to all of its codes, beliefs, and allegiances. Sometimes jumping in involves being beaten up by other gang members in a kind of ritual that tests endurance and provides a few moments of close physical contact. Getting jumped out of a gang usually involves a worse, more vengeful beating that may result in death.

Machismo. A code and set of values for male behavior and male identity. This code of manliness specifies courage, a lack of emotional expression, competition, and physical strength. It often defines women's roles narrowly, expecting them to take on the sole identities of girlfriends, wives, or mothers who provide food, sex, and a comfortable home and who obey the orders of their male partners.

Nation. A loose confederation of gangs, sometimes stretching across the country. The Crips, the Bloods, and the Folk are examples of gang nations.

Turf. Territory in a neighborhood, town, or city that a gang claims as its own. The gang conducts most of its operations on its "turf." These activities can include meetings, drug-dealing, control of neighborhood businesses, and socializing. In many cases, members of other gangs are not even expected to walk through this territory. Neighboring gangs are often in constant struggle to enlarge the boundaries of their turf. Turf wars are one of the main causes of gang-banging.

Vendetta. Gang vengeance. Vendettas are part of the code of the gang lifestyle. If a gang member is slighted, physically hurt, or killed, then the offending party must suffer. Those who undertake vendettas often speak of life as if it were a balance sheet in which the wrongs done to either party have to be equal. Most vendettas cause endless chains of violence. The wronged party always wants a new vendetta to shift the balance.

INDEX

A

Alanon, 64
alcoholism, 61, 64, 87
Almighty Black P. Stones gang, 74
Amer-I-Can program, 77, 78
angel dust, 66, 69
anti-gang programs, 77, 78-83, 85-86
Aryan White Knights, 29
Asian gangs, 55-59
Atlantic Union College, 79

B

"beating in," 7
Birmingham, Ala., 29-30
black gangs, 31, 68
Blackstone Rangers gang, 74, 75
Bloods gang, 7, 8, 73, 76
    history of, 74-75
    feud with Crips, 76
Bluitt, Michael, 81
Boston Film-Video Foundation, 79
Brentwood, Cal., 33, 34
Brown, Jim, 77, 78

C

Chicanos, 20, 24, 33
Chinatown, New York City, 55-59
clothing styles, 39, 41-43, 44, 47, 52, 87
codes of behavior, 45-47, 52-53
colors, 9, 12, 39, 41-43, 44, 45, 81
Confederate Hammer Skinheads, 29, 31
crack cocaine, 59-61, 64, 69, 75, 76
"crews," 11
"cribs," 39
Crips gang, 7, 47, 73, 74, 78
    feud with Bloods, 76

D

Dailey, Rodney, 78-79
Davis, Gregory, 78
Diamond Heights gang, 19-27, 33, 89
drive-by shootings, 7, 9, 61, 75
drug addiction, 11, 59, 66-68, 71
drug dealing, 46, 56, 57, 59-65, 68-71, 75
Drug Enforcement Administration (DEA), 57

E

El Rukns gang, 68

F

family problems, 14, 26, 87
Federal Bureau of Investigation (FBI), 82
Feliciano, Maribel, 43
female gangs, 13
Folk Nation gang, 7, 31
Fort Worth, Tex., 80

G

Galleon, Adam, 31
gambling, 56, 57-58
Gang Peace program, 78-79
gangs
    Asian, 55-59
    avoiding, 86-88
    charters, 45, 59, 74
    clothing, 39, 41-43, 44, 47, 52, 87
    codes of behavior, 45-47, 52-53
    colors, 9, 12, 39, 41-43, 44, 45, 81
    definitions of, 9, 11, 13
    drug trade and, 59-65, 66-71
    female, 13
    "jumping out," 73, 85-86
    leaving, 85-86
    prison, 11, 68, 81
    reasons for joining, 13-17
    skinhead, 29-35
    street, 11
    tattoos, 8, 39, 40-41, 45, 78, 87
    truces, 78-80, 83
    vendettas, 48-51, 53
    Vietnamese, 58
Georgetown University, 47
Germany, Betty J., 47
Ghost Shadow gang, 55-56, 58-59
graffiti, 78, 81
guns, 16, 69, 75
    deaths from, 45

H

Harbor Area Gang Alternatives Program, 81
Hartford, Conn., 35-36